How To Meditate:

Practicing Mindfulness & Meditation to Reduce Stress, Anxiety & Find Lasting Happiness Even if You Are Not Religious, a Beginner or Experienced

Meditation
Checklist

Use this simple checklist to make sure you have The Most Powerful Meditation Every Time

FIND OUT MORE

Table of Contents

References

Introduction

Mindfulness has always been a big deal in human history. However, its importance in the frantic nature of the modern world cannot be overemphasized. In *The 7 Habits of Highly Effective People* by Stephen Covey, a particular statement popped out of the book and has always been on my mind. He used an illustration in which a person was driving so fast that his tires had to be punctured to gain his attention.

Stephen Covey used this illustration to explain how **you should not move through life so fast that your "tires have to be punctured" to get your attention.** In other words, you don't need a disaster before you start paying attention to important things in your life. Unfortunately, so many people are entrenched in the fast lane of life because of the pressure from work and other things. It is good to be ambitious in life to achieve your dreams but it should not be at any cost.

When I mentioned "disaster", I am talking about unfortunate events such as the loss of a loved one or a decline in health. It is so sad that a lot of people only realize how important their health is when they have terminal diseases or psychotic diseases. In the same way, some people never learn to value their relationships until they lose them either by death or divorce. Many people claim to be too busy to take care of their physical and psychological health but will be forced to pay attention to it when things go wrong.

Some also claim to have a schedule that is so busy that it prevents them from spending quality time with their loved ones. They will only regret when they lose these precious people in the long run. However, you can avoid getting caught in the web or running too fast in life by inculcating the habit of meditation. Mindfulness is not only beneficial to your health but also to your performance in your daily activities.

Mindfulness is a simple but powerful tool that will enable you to live a happy and fulfilled life. Many people chase money so long in their lives only to realize that what they really need is happiness and fulfillment. They think money will give them happiness and fulfillment but they realized that they were wrong eventually. I am not saying that wealth and happiness are mutually exclusive; I am only addressing your priority.

Mindfulness is the process through which you focus our mind on specific things. You are alert and conscious of events in your life and deliberate about making changes where necessary. Most people are victims and products of the circumstances in their lives. However, mindfulness puts you in charge of your life. It enables you to pay attention to the minute but important details that can transform your life.

Just the same way a car has to stop and get fuel to be able to complete a journey; you need mindfulness as a person. Only those who have experienced the vitality and freshness that comes from meditation can fully explain its power. You have to take out time mediate to make your journey in life smother. There is a limit to your level of effectiveness when you keep huffing and puffing. You need to relax your soul adequately and start afresh again to get new ideas and be reinvigorated.

There are a couple of times when your mind will go through some things but you are distracted by the matters at hand. Meditation gives you a bird view of your life in which you have all the angles covered. In mindfulness, you are in "flight mode"; your mind is the focal point as you lose sight of your body. It empowers you to realize how powerful you are and have a proper view of your potentials. The resultant effect of this realization is that you will no longer be anxious and afraid about facing your daily challenges.

The benefits of mindfulness are endless and you will learn more about them as you continue to read this book. Ultimately, the transformative effect of mindfulness will enable you to live and happy and fulfilled life. Therefore, this educative book was written and compiled to lead you through the process of living a fuller and happy life. You will learn all that you need to know about meditation beginning in history and how to go about it.

This book is a complete guide that will help you either as a beginner or veteran of mindfulness. No information was left out including the kind of clothes you should wear when practicing mindfulness. This book is the solution to both ignorance and misconceptions about meditation. There are benefits some people think they will get through meditation which are not actually true. You will learn more as you progress on this memorable journey.

You only live once and you need to commit yourself to anything that will add value to your experience as a person. You have made the right choice by reading this book because it will definitely add value to your life. However, how much value you will get from reading this book depends on your attitude. If you have a casual approach to the study of this book, you will get the kind of effect a casual study deserved – no effect.

I am sure that you have other things to do with your time before you decided to commit to reading this book. Hence, you have to be determined to get the best out of the study of this book. Ensure you study this book deliberately to improve the quality of your life. The adequate research that produced this book guarantees the high quality of its content. Hence, the ball is in your court to study your way into good health and a happy and fulfilled life.

Chapter One: Finding Your Why/Purpose of Meditation

Only an unreasonable person will participate in an activity that he or she does not have any reason for participation. I know you are not an unreasonable person and that is why it is very vital that I intimate you with the reason for meditation. Just like every positive activity in life, you will have reasons to be discouraged to continue this new path.

However, what will keep on motivating you are the benefits you stand to gain by consistent and deliberate practice of meditation. Hence, in this chapter, I will be taking you through the importance of meditation to your life both in the short-term and long-term. The understanding of these benefits will help you maintain your focus in the long run.

The Monkey Mind

The "Monkey Mind" is an eastern idea that originated from Buddhism. I know the idea of possessing the mind of a monkey sounds funny but the reality and implications are critical. The monkey mind refers to a state of mind that is restless, uncontrollable, indecisive, and confused. The truth is that we all have a Monkey Mind and you must learn to subdue it for optimal performance.

You have myriads of thoughts running through your mind all day. While you are thinking about your car, you quickly switch to your spouse or kids. You were trying to think about a party, and then you suddenly remember that your exams are coming up the week after the party. The list goes on and on and it is not every time that your thoughts are on different topics.

Sometimes, this to and fro swinging action of your mind is around different parts of the same topic. For example, you may be thinking about how to be a better parent to your kid and switch in no time to what you need to do for your first son when he is back from school. We all have to battle this state of being unsettled on a particular thought for long just like a monkey swinging from one branch of a tree to the other.

Each thought is like a branch of a tree. It may sound fun to you in your imagination of a swinging monkey enjoying its day. However, in reality in the human context, it impairs your performance. You need to be able to concentrate on a thought for a while to be able to make a decisive decision that will be beneficial in the long run. Hence, it is critical to know how to control your thoughts to improve your experiences in life.

Meditation or mindfulness is the remedy for the malady of a monkey mind. Meditation is a positive version of worry. Worry brings with it irrational fears of losing your job or inability to satisfy your spouse or be a responsible parent to your kids. You will end up becoming mentally drained and you will often find out in the long run that it was never worth it.

Hence, you will have to learn to decrease the volume of the chattering monkey in your mind to focus on ways of improving your life. There are many ways you can get better as a person but you will struggle to focus on them when your monkey mind is in full motion. You need to slow down and maintain perfect tranquility within yourself to make headway in your life. There is no better way to have that inner peace than the serenity of mindfulness.

Benefits of consistent meditation

There are many advantages you stand to enjoy when you inculcate the habit of subduing your monkey mind via meditation. Below are the benefits of consistent meditation:

Reduced Stress and Depression

According to the World Health Organization (W.H.O), over 300 million people of all ages over the world are suffering from depression. Depression is a major contributor to the problem of ailments all over the world. The W.H.O reckons that it is the leading cause of disability all over the world. At its peak, depression can make people commit suicide. There are various therapies to help people who suffer from depression but prevention is always better than cure.

Stress is another main malaise many people in the world handle. The nature of the modern world makes it impossible to totally eradicate stress. However, you can effectively manage your stress level to an acceptable degree. Various researches have been able to establish that mindfulness can mitigate the effect of stress and depression.

Fang Lu and his colleagues carried out research in 2019 among 500 Chinese intensive nurses. The research showed that mindfulness negates the effect of stress on emotional exhaustion including depression. Hence, mindfulness is never a waste of time. It is vital to cut down stress levels and prevent depression. Depression is a problem people of all age categories and social status face.

Hence, don't assume that the reason you are depressed is simply that you don't have enough money. When you practice mindfulness, you will realize that there are so many things in your life more worthwhile than money. Your worth will not be based on ephemeral things but enduring values like your relationships and contributions to the lives of people around you.

Increased Calmness and Clarity of Thought

Mindfulness offers your soul unparallel serenity and tranquility. Many people live life with such a frantic pace that makes them susceptible to making poor decisions. Whether you like it or not, you cannot deny that the best decisions you have made in your life were during moments when you were not under pressure. The problem is that people and circumstances around you will make it difficult to make decisions without pressure.

However, the ball is in your court because only you have the right to choose the way you want your life to go. If any person has an influence on the decisions you make in life, it is because you gave them that privilege. Hence, unless it is absolutely necessary, don't make a decision without thinking it through. Most critical life decisions such as your career path or choice of life partner should not be made at the spur of the moment.

Mindfulness offers you the clarity of thought that will enable you to make wise decisions. Many do not admit it but the calmness of mind it a critical attribute anyone can possess. Calmness and patience are strengths that many views as "sluggishness" in the modern world. However, that assertion is false in practice.

Fewer Mistakes at Work and in Your Social Life

The product of a calm and clear state of mind is quality decision-making. The resultant effect of quality decision-making is that you will make fewer mistakes in your private and social life. You will also reduce the error of judgment at work and that will improve your performance. You are an active individual who will have to make decisions about various aspects of your life every day. It is essential that you make the right decisions consistently.

I am not implying that you have to be perfect because that is impossible. It is not possible that you will not make mistakes at all in your life. In the words of Life is a long journey in which you will make mistakes and learn from them. However, every mistake will cost you. Sometimes the damage is minimal but there are times the damage can be devastating. Hence, you have to ensure you make fewer mistakes in your daily activities. You can take advantage of consistent meditation to offer you're the fulcrum to make quality decisions and reduce the rate of errors in your life.

Focus and Clarity of Purpose

Focus and clarity of purpose are vital ingredients that will enable you to achieve your dream in life. Experts reckon that a dream is not yet a dream until it is specific, measurable, achievable, relevant, and time-bound. Hence, you have not begun until you have that specific goal you want to achieve in life. It takes a calm mind and clarity of purpose to set specific goals you want to achieve in your life.

When you live life with your monkey mind getting the better of you, you will swing from one dream to the other. You will only do what seems to appeal to you at a particular time. Your dream will be nothing but a product of current trends and turn of events. You need clarity of purpose to have a dream but that is not enough to achieve your dream.

You will face various challenges that will make you want to back down from attaining your goal. You will have many reasons to give up because of various distractions. Hence, beyond the clarity of purpose, the focus is very vital for you to be able to reach your destination. Mindfulness enables you to have clarity of purpose and focus required to achieve your dream in life. Hence, mindfulness is an important practice for those who want to make the best out of their lives.

Happiness and Enjoyment of the Present Moment

There are many pursuits of people in life but we all ultimately just want to be happy. You strive daily to earn more money, be a better parent, friend, and spouse. However, these pursuits are a means to the ultimate need of man – happiness. Many people think that happiness is a product of circumstances when it is actually a deliberate choice you make.

One of the ways you can choose to be happy is to choose to enjoy the present moment. During mindfulness, you lose sight of fear and worry and focus on reasons to be happy. There will always be reasons to be sad but there are also reasons to be happy. Hence, your happiness depends on you. The inner strength you need to focus on the positive aspects of your life and be optimistic about the future comes from meditation.

Chapter Two: Origins

It is not out of place to wonder where mindfulness came from. There is nothing in this world that does not have a beginning somewhere and mindfulness is not different. The journey of the practice of mindfulness began in the East before finding its way to the West. In this chapter, we will be looking at the background of the practice of meditation. I will be tasking you through how it all began; the evolution, and current modern trend. The essence of this brief history is to help you appreciate the preservation of this practice all through human history.

Mindfulness in recent times has enjoyed widespread acceptance among nonreligious people in the West. Various religions from Buddhism and Hinduism have practiced mindfulness for thousands of years before it began to gain acceptance among people who do not practice Hinduism or Buddhism. Basically, the practice of meditation was made popular in the East by religious institutions but made popular in the West by individuals and institutions.

However, the practice of mindfulness in the West can be traced to Eastern Origins. Hence, it is safe to say that mindfulness is a practice that began in the East that also became popular in the West. However, it is important to note that mindfulness is not only a practice found in the two aforementioned religions – Hinduism and Buddhism. It can also be found in religions such as Islam, Christianity, and Judaism.

According to Trousselard and his colleagues (2014), some commentators in history argue that Hinduism and Buddhism should not take the center stage when it comes to mindfulness because it is also prominent in Islam, Christianity, and Judaism. However, it is impossible to deny that most modern practitioners of mindfulness in the West learned about it from Hindu and Buddhists tradition. Hence, the focal point of this historical background is Hindu and Buddhist traditions.

Brief History of Buddhism

Unlike Hinduism, Buddhism has a well-defined history. It was founded by Buddha (Siddhartha Gautama) around 400-500 B.C.E. It is believed that Buddha was born and raised in India. There are many similarities between Hinduism and Buddhism and Hinduism is believed to have influenced the upbringing of Buddha. Both Hinduism and Buddhism are concerned about *Dharma* and are both from the same region.

"Dharma" is a concept that is not easy to explain but has to do with the harmony of life with the natural order of the universe. According to Hacker and Davis (2006), Buddhism is not a subsect of Hinduism in spite of the similarities. A key difference between these two religions is that unlike Hinduism, Buddhism does not focus on the ancient writings of the Veda. The aim of Buddhism is to enlighten its followers. The path to enlightenment was what inspired Buddha to begin his search and Buddhism is the product of his findings and teachings.

There are many factions in Buddhism and it began even when Buddha was still alive. Various traditions of Buddhism include *Zen Buddhism* and *Theravada Buddhism*. Most people who do not practice Buddhism view it in the light of Tibetan Buddhism and an enlightened teacher of Tibetan Buddhism called the *Dalai Lama*. Zen Buddhism began in China during the Tang Dynasty and it was called the Chan School back then before it later developed into different schools.

Zen Buddhism places a premium on intuitive knowledge which is a knowledge that is not based on reality but a gut feeling. The most commonly accepted name of the old extant name of Buddhism is Theravada. The Theravada school base their belief and practice on the teachings of Gautama Buddha. Tibetan Buddhism as formed from the blending of Buddhism with Tibetan religion.

Just like many religions, there is a whole lot of philosophy in Buddhism. Mindfulness is more entrenched in Buddhism than Hinduism. In Buddhism, mindfulness is considered as the first step towards enlightenment. Enlightenment is the process of viewing your original mind without the use of your intellect. Western mindfulness owes a lot to Buddhism because most people who made the practice popular in the West were tutored by Buddhist teachers.

Brief History of Hinduism

Just like Buddhism, Hinduism is one of the widely accepted religions among the oldest extant religion in the world. Though it is called a religion in the West, in the East, they prefer to call it "a way of life" or "dharma". With over 900 million followers in the world, Hinduism is the third-largest religion in the world only behind Islam and Christianity. It is considered to be the oldest of all the oldest extant religion but without a clear history like Buddhism.

The reason for this unclear history is that Hinduism is a product of the blending of various religions in the regions that formed modern India. Therefore, apparently, there is no particular founder of Hinduism unlike Buddhism. In fact, no one called the Religion "Hinduism" until in the 1800s when British writers referred to Vedic traditions as Hinduism. Over 4000 years ago, the gem form of Hinduism was prevalent in the Indus valley - modern-day Pakistan. These traditions are now part and parcel of Hinduism.

The development of these traditions did not stop in Vedic writings 2500-3500 years ago. The devotion to common Gods and the rituals observed in Hinduism in the modern world are in these writings. Additional texts were written about 1500-2500 years ago and these writings are still relevant in the modern practice of the religion. These writings include temple worship as well as the concept of dharma which is also present in Buddhism. Islam became a major competition with Hinduism in recent times. However, the effort of 19th-century reformers ensured that Hinduism became identified as a religion that denotes the national heritage of India.

The 19th-century reformers achieved their aims and a benchmark for their success is the identification of middle-class Indians in particular with the religion in mid 19th century (Hatcher, 2007). The Indian independence movement further solidified the belief of Indians in Hinduism. Although it not as pronounced as Buddhism, meditation has been involved in the practice of Hinduism for years. Hence, it is not possible to talk about the history of mindfulness and not say anything about the history of Hinduism. Both mindfulness and Buddhism are indebted to Hinduism. Meditation is found in the discussions of Bhagavad Gita of Yoga as well as Vedic meditation.

Mindfulness and Yoga

Many people think mindfulness and Yoga are the same but that is not the case. Mindfulness is incorporated in Yoga practices but not the same as Yoga. Yoga is a broader practice that includes various aspects as well as mindfulness. However, mindfulness is an integral part of yoga practices. Historically and presently, there is a lot of overlap between Yoga practices and mindfulness meditation practices. Body scan, for example, is common to both mindfulness and yoga practices.

Gaiswinkler and Unterrainer (2016) measured "mindfulness" among people who practice yoga. The essence of this measurement is to examine the similarities between yoga and mindfulness practices. The result of the study showed that those who were slightly involved in yoga had a lower level of mindfulness than people who were regularly involved in yoga practices. The implication of this result is that there is a positive correlation between yoga and mindfulness.

The result also implies that some forms of mindfulness and some forms of yoga are aiming towards achieving the same objective. It is also interesting to notice that the origins of Hinduism coincide with the origins of yoga. Besides, mindfulness began to gain ascendancy and popularity in the West the same period yoga started becoming popular in the West. These seeming coincidences show that Hinduism, Buddhism, yoga, and mindfulness practices are intertwined and interrelated.

The Journey of Mindfulness from the East to the West

Jon Kabat-Zinn is credited with the biggest influence as regards bringing mindfulness to the West. He was the founder of the Center for Mindfulness at the University of Massachusetts' Medical School. He was also the founder of the Oasis Institute for Mindfulness-Based Professional Education and Training. He developed an eight-week program for reducing stress which he called "Mindfulness-Based Stress Reduction (MSSR)" program.

The MSSR program was developed at the Oasis Institute for Mindfulness-Based Professional Education and Training.

Kabat-Zin gathered his knowledge from various Buddhist teachers. These teachers include the influential and popular Thich Nhat Hanh. Thich Nhat Hanh is a popular figure when it comes to Western mindfulness practices. Hence, Kabat-Zin was given an Eastern foundation upon which he developed the MSSR program.

It was the integration of Eastern philosophies with Western Science by Kabat-Zin that made mindfulness popular in the West. There is another mindfulness-based therapy called "Mindfulness-based Cognitive Therapy" (MBCT). The MBCT is a therapy developed for the purpose of treating Major Depressive Disorder. The MBCT was inspired by Kabat-Zin's MSSR. For people who were only familiar with Western science but not Easter practices, Kabat-Zin's work became a reference point thereby increasing the popularity of mindfulness in the West.

The reason it took Kabat-Zin, a Westerner to popularize an Eastern practice in the West is because of the differences in perception in these two regions. An example of such differences is an individualistic worldview that is prevalent in the West and an Institutional mindset prevalent in the East. There were other people apart from Kabat-Zin who also played crucial roles in the popularity of mindfulness in the West.

Sharon Salzberg, Jack Kornfield, and Joseph Goldstein contributed to the popularity of mindfulness in the West. They contributed by establishing the Insight Meditation Society (IMS) in 1975. This foundation introduced and popularized mindfulness meditation to both clinical and non-clinical populations. There are many other institutions apart from the IMS that made meditation popular in the West but they stand out among the rest.

Positive psychology is an aspect of psychology that is focused on the happiness of man. Mindfulness is a crucial tool used by positive psychologists to develop therapies that will make life better for people. MBCT is one of such therapies and it has wide acceptance among psychologists as an effective therapy to treat various patients. Hence, mindfulness is more than just a practice but a scientifically proven method of improving the quality of your life.

More people in the West are embracing meditation as a practice to help them live a happy and meaningful life. There are scientific evidences that validate the claims of people who believe mindfulness helps people to make the best out of their lives. Positive results abound to the effect of proving that mindfulness is not a farce but the real deal. In the subsequent chapters, you will gain more insight into the power and method of practicing mindfulness.

Chapter Three: The Power of Mindfulness

So, far, we have been able to explore the importance or benefit of meditation in your life. We have also been able to examine a brief history as regards how mindfulness came from the East and became popular in the West. However, we have not discussed what meditation really is. What is the power of meditation? You know the benefits you stand to enjoy through mindfulness. More so, it should interest you to know what mindfulness is really all about.

In this chapter, we will explore the meaning of mindfulness as well as what makes it effective. We will also explore how you can become better as you practice mindfulness consistently as well as the importance of breathing in meditation.

What is Mindfulness?

Mindfulness is not all about being mindful which will literarily mean to be careful or cautious. It is not a restrictive term for self-imprisonment or consignment as some think. Instead, mindfulness involves the training of your mind to bring it to a state of stillness. It is the process of making your mind focus on what it should focus on. So many times in life, you know you are being distracted and allowing your mind to wander just like a monkey jumping from branch to branch.

Mindfulness is a psychological process in which you deliberately bring your focus on the current situation. Being able to concentrate on the present moment is not an automatic process but something you achieve through training. It takes deliberate and consistent mindfulness practice before you can prevent your mind from wandering into the future or the past.

Thinking about the future is not wrong but you may worry and fear irrationally because of pessimism about the future. It is not also wrong to think about the past but it can bring with it guilt about things you didn't do well in the past.

Mindfulness is a derivative of *sati* which is a crucial element of Buddhist traditions. It is based on Tibetan, Vipassana, and Zen meditation techniques. Mindlessness is the opposite of mindfulness. Mindlessness can be explained by those moments when you eat and suddenly realize you have just a couple left. You have been eating but not enjoying the moment. It is a state of being on autopilot mode. It sounds like fun but it is dangerous.

An example of research that shows that most people leave their minds on autopilot is the research carried out by Matt Killingsworth. He created an app with which he derived opinions about what makes people happy the most. In a sampling of 15,000 people across different socio demographic variables, the result was outstanding. The result of the research showed that people are most happy when they mindful of the moment and are not happy when they let their minds wander about. According to experts, an autopilot mode is just like being in a dream where you are not aware of your present condition.

When you are on autopilot, you will not notice the beauty of the world around you. Life will lose color to you and everything seems to be passing away right in front of you. In this state, you are no longer living but merely existing. Mindfulness involves taking the steering wheel and be the one directing your thoughts and your life. Mindfulness involves maintaining a moment-by-moment awareness of what goes on in your mind, the way you feel, and the sensations in your surroundings.

The Power of the Mind

Your mind is such a crucial part of your life that you cannot afford to handle with levity. In the Book of Proverbs in the Bible, King Solomon counseled that you should guard your heart (mind) with all diligence because therein lies the issues of life. Your mind is the steering wheel of your life and you have to be the one in charge. The terrible thing about the mind is that when you are not in charge of it, it will be on autopilot mode. It is never static but dynamic and relentless. It can move from stillness to chaos within a short period.

You know you have so much potential but you are finding it to unlock your undisputed ability. The late Miles Munroe stated that the richest place on earth is not the oil wells of the Arabs but the graveyard. The statement is intriguing and awkward at the same time but the truth is not farfetched. He was referring to great potentials that were never discovered or utilized before the possessor died. So many bestseller books, record-breaking movies, revolutionary speeches, and great business ideas worth billions of dollars have died with many people.

Hence, I agree with him that the graveyard is the richest place on earth. You are still alive (obviously that is why you can read this book) and you still have so many opportunities to make the world a better place. However, you cannot change the world until you change yourself. You have to break free from some routines and begin new ones to change your experience in life. Every great thing that has ever been achieved on earth begins from the mind of a person or group of people. Hence, your mind is the most vital part of your life. The Buddha says it all:

"To enjoy good health, to bring true happiness to one's family, to bring peace to all, one must first discipline and control one's mind. If a man can control his mind, he can find

the way to Enlightenment, and all wisdom and virtue will naturally come to him".

The direction of your life depends on the direction of your mind. Before you take a step, your mind has conceived it. Hence, you can never be greater than what goes on in your mind. Circumstances in life tend to make you want to focus on negative thoughts and limitations you have. It is true that you have limitations and we all do. However, you have so much strength as well but you will never be able to harness your strength when you don't put your mind in order. Control your mind and you will be able to control your life.

That requisite control you need to avoid your mind being in autopilot mode is what meditation offers to you. Once your mind spirals out of control, you have lost the plot. People who give up on life and commit suicide got to that point they should never get to. They allowed their mind to spiral out of control. They allowed their thoughts to drive them to make a terrible irreversible decision. There are many things that can go wrong when you are not in charge and you should never let that happen. Thankfully, meditation is a gift from the universe to rescue us.

What You Practice Grows Stronger

The most important thing about meditation practices is getting started. Don't allow procrastination to deprive you of what you stand to enjoy via mindfulness practices. You don't need to be perfect to start. It is perfect when you decide to start. Every great thing begins with a step. Rome was not built in a day after all. Hence, what is more important is starting first and not being bothered about doing it well. The more you practice, the stronger and better you will become over time. According to Nicole Byer:

"What can cake teach you about life? That practice makes perfect, and if you try something once, it probably won't be perfect, and you have to keep working on it if you want to be good at it."

I need to sound a note of warning that mindfulness is not some kind of magic wand. Most people want something they can just do within a day or two and their lives will transform radically in a positive way. However, there is no such thing as that. It is an accumulation of little efforts here and there that ends up deciding what happens in your life in the long run. A great man is seen in his daily routines. It is little drops of water that ends up becoming an ocean with patience.

Hence, don't feel discouraged if it feels as if you are not getting concrete result within a few days of practicing mindfulness. I am not saying that you cannot get immediate results by practicing mindfulness. However, it is not always like that for everybody. The truth is that positive changes are already taking place in your life from the day you start practicing mindfulness. However, it may not be obvious to you yet. Hence, don't give up because you are not having your expectations met yet. Don't give up and you will be glad you didn't eventually.

Breathing

Breathing is an integral part of meditation. Meditation involves paying attention to your own breath. You need to set out time because an interruption is the last thing you need to practice "mindful breathing". 15 minutes is more than enough to do this daily. However, you can set out more time as you practice and reap the benefits. What do you stand to gain? You will have a reduction in stress, anxiety level and focus on what matters.

You don't have to practice meditative breathing only during the designated time. You can also practice it when you are feeling stressed and under intense pressure to cool yourself down. However, practicing meditative breathing during difficult moments is not automatic; it comes with practice. The more you practice it during periods when you are calm, the more you will be able to use it during tough times. During tough times, you can start by taking a very deep breath and hold it for like three seconds before you exhale through your nostrils. With mouth, you can make it four seconds.

Breathing during meditation is as simple as focusing on inhaling and exhaling. You can stand while doing this or sit down. You can also lie down as long as you are comfortable. There are differences here and there and you will discover what works best for you over time. A little trial and error initially will not do any harm. You can also close your eyes because it is easier to maintain your focus that way. However, if you don't want to close your eyes, you can simply look at the ground or stare into space.

As you breathe and try to focus on your breath, you will find your mind wander and distracted by your thoughts and body sensations. Don't fight it; just gently bring your attention back to your breath. Stay there for like seven minutes and get lost in your breath and your thought and then your breathing again. Before you stop, relax and observe your body and savor your effort and discipline.

Chapter Four: The Technique of Meditation

There are techniques involved in the practice of meditation. Failure to do it the right way will prevent you from getting the best result out of the practice. Whatever is worth doing at all should be given the requisite attention and effort to get the best out of it. Hence, when it comes to meditation, it is important you are conversant with important things as regards how to go about it. In this chapter, I will be helping you with the different ways you can meditate and still get similar results. You will also learn about what to wear and other beneficial information that will take you from a novice to a pro in meditation.

Different Ways to Meditate

There are different meditation practices and each one requires its own peculiar mental skills. Below are the different ways to meditate:

Concentration Meditation

Concentration meditation is important, especially for beginners. It involves focusing on a particular thing or point. You may focus on your breath or a particular word or mantra. You can also consider looking intensely at a candle flame or any other activity that can distract you from the thoughts on your mind. It is easier said than done for a beginner and you will need to be happy with the progress you are making. You may only be able to meditate for a few minutes initially before you are able to do it for longer periods.

Don't feel disappointed in yourself; be happy with the fact that you are doing all you can do get better. If you don't give up, you will be impressed with your level of improvement. This form of meditation is all about training your mind to focus instead of wandering from one thought to the other. Hence, you have to make up your mind about what exactly you want to focus on all through the period of meditation. Failure to decide what you want to focus on before you start meditating will lead to chasing various thoughts.

Don't overestimate yourself because your mind can become boisterous in no time. Therefore, to avoid fighting a needless battle with your thoughts, decide what you want to be the focal point of your attention while meditating. Ensure what you want to focus on is not vague such that your attention drifts away from it over time. It is always better to choose something physical like the flame of a candle rather than a thought. Focusing on a particular thought is feasible but it is not easy. Your best bet is something you can look at or listen to in order to get the best out of concentration meditation.

Mindfulness Meditation

Mindfulness meditation is not as rigid as concentration meditation. This technique of meditation involves actually allowing your mind to wander. However, this wandering is to the end that you can monitor every mental note as it arises. The intention is not to judge your thoughts or scrutinize them but to be aware of your thought pattern. It is more like being in the position of an eagle observing the activities of chicks on the ground except that you will never interfere at any point.

This observation of your thought pattern and tendencies will give a clear view of how your mind drifts so that you can know how to curb and direct it. Mindfulness meditation will let you see how you judge various experiences as worthwhile or useless. Mindfulness meditation will eventually help you develop an inner balance for your thought pattern in the long run. Some schools of meditation combine both the concentration and mindfulness meditation techniques. Whether it is mindfulness or concentration meditation technique, what matters is discipline and stillness to focus on the activities going in your mind.

Cultivation of Compassion

Cultivation of techniques is not a common meditation technique but it is nonetheless effective. It is a technique found among Buddhist monks. It involves a deliberate imagination of negative circumstances and recasting them in a positive light to cultivate compassion. This technique is not pessimism or an expectation of unpleasant events. Cultivation of compassion is about imagining negative events and how you will handle them in a positive way. Hence, this technique is all about being proactive rather than being reactive.

No one wants to experience unpleasant situations such as betrayal or a cheating spouse. However, such occurrences are part and parcel of life that happens to even the best of us all. However, you can choose to forgive people when you see their offenses as "frailties of human beings". When you see the offenses of people that way, you will be able to have compassion and forgive them. Cultivation of compassion helps you to prepare your mind for such terrible experiences and be strong in case they happen.

What to wear

The knowledge of what you should wear during meditation is as important as the knowledge of the techniques of meditation. In fact, knowing what to wear in itself is an important technique in meditation. What you wear lays the foundation and sets the tone for how much you will get out of your meditation. You have to be mindful of the effect of your cloth on people around you if you are meditating in a public place. The color of the cloth you pick also matters because it can either support or negate the purpose of your meditation.

Wear Comfortable Outfits

The first thing you need to consider when picking what to wear during meditation is the comfort of the cloth. You should wear an outfit that is comfortable and makes you feel confident. There is really no such thing as wrong clothing especially when you meditate at the comfort of your room. You can even meditate without wearing any cloth as long as you are alone in your room. However, you will have people around you, then, you need comfortable yoga pants, sweat pants, and tank tops.

Avoid Wearing Tight-fitting Clothes

You should avoid wearing tight-fitting clothes when meditating because they will hinder your breathing. Wear loose clothing that will enable you to breathe comfortably while mediating. It is important to note that wearing something loose does not imply that you should wear a gown or any other cloth that will get in the way. However, a flowing robe can be utilized. If you are feeling numb in your legs during meditation, it may be a sign that your clothes are too tight. Pants with elastic pants are good options because they offer no restriction regardless of the position of meditation.

Go for the Right Color

The color of your outfit also matters. Every color has its own energy. Hence, the purpose of the meditation will determine the color of your outfit. The color red stands for courage and strength and encourages physical activity. Yellow engenders intellect, happiness, and creativity. White is the color of virtue and protection while green encourages prosperity and healing. Therefore, if you have health challenges, you should wear green when meditating. In the same way, you should wear a yellow outfit if you are having issues with depression.

Other Tips

In case you want to go and meditate in a temple, you have to be courteous because there are often restrictions and rules you need to obey. Hence, to avoid the embarrassment of being asked to go back because you are not dressing appropriately, it is better you call someone who can give you accurate information as regards the dress code. Usually, the restrictions are usually around not wearing something too short and seductive.

You can also consider layering your cloth. Layering your cloth will ensure that you are comfortable regardless of the environment you choose to meditate. Initially, you may feel cold but you will feel warm later. If there is an air conditioner where you intend to meditate, you can use a hoodie or light jacket. You can also get some socks to avoid getting cold in case you have to be barefoot.

Meditating Positions

Whether you are sitting, standing, lying down, or kneeling, there is a way to go about it when meditating. Below are helpful tips that will help you with each meditation position:

Chair-sitting Meditation

Chair sitting meditation is ideal for meditating while at work or while travelling. The right position for chair-sitting meditation is to sit straight back in your chair with your feet flat on the floor. Your feet should form a 90-degree angle with knees and you may need to scoot to the edge of the chair to achieve this. Your sitting position should be such that your head and your neck are in line with your spine while sitting straight. For additional support, you can employ the use of a pillow. Place it under your hips or behind your lower back. As for your hands, just place them on your laps or on your knees.

Standing Meditation

In case you are not comfortable with sitting meditation, you can consider standing meditation. Standing meditation involves standing tall with your feet shoulder-width apart. Turn your heels slightly inward by shifting your feet such that your toes are slightly pointing away from each other. Bend your knees slightly when you are in a position. With every exhale, let your body root down through your feet. Have an image of the lifting of your energy through the crown of your head each time you inhale. Place your hands on your belly to feel your breath moving through your body for additional relaxation.

Kneeling Meditation

Kneeling meditation is ideal if you are somewhere you can kneel down comfortably. The advantage of kneeling meditation is that it makes it easy for you to keep your back straight. This meditation position involves bending your knees as you rest on the floor. Your ankles should be below your bottom while shins are flat on the ground. For additional support, place a cushion between heels and your bottom. This will help you to avoid straining your knees. If you feel pain while meditating in this position, you should try another position but you should not feel pain normally. To avoid putting too much pressure on your knees, root your weight back and down through your hips.

Lying-down Meditation

Relaxation and release of tension are easier with lying down meditation. This meditation position supports your body totally. This meditation position involves lying on your back while your arms are extended alongside your body. Turn your toes to the side while your feet are hip-distance apart. Modify the pose to support your lower back if you are not feeling comfortable. When lying flat, place a pillow underneath your knees to slightly elevate them.

Using essential oils

Essential oils have nutritional value but can also be used to good effect in meditation practices. Your serenity and sense of calm during meditation can improve greatly with the use of essential oils. Essential oils commonly used during meditation include Patchouli, Vetiver, Palo Santo, Cedarwood, and Atlas. These essential oils are considered grounding. Other essential oils such as Roman Chamomile, Clary Sage, and Lavender are considered to have the ability to enhance the state of relaxation as well as act as natural sedatives.

There are some essential oils that have the ability to enhance spiritual connection with the divine. They include Frankincense and Helichrysum. You can also combine different essential oils to create a blend of their abilities. For the purpose of blending, a candle diffuser or a room mist can be utilized. It is important to note that you should understand the contraindications and safety of every essential oil before you use it.

To create a relaxation blend, you can combine 3 parts of lavender with 2 parts Atlas and 1 part Bergamot. For an enlightening blend, go for a combination of Frankincense and Helichrysum according to the manufacturer's instruction. The combination of Frankincense, Sandalwood, and Bergamot will produce a good grounding blend.

To create a relaxation blend, you can combine 3 parts of lavender with 2 parts Atlas and 1 part Bergamot. For an enlightening blend, go for a combination of Frankincense and Helichrysum according to the manufacturer's instruction. The combination of Frankincense, Sandalwood, and Bergamot will produce a good grounding blend.

Chapter Five: Body Scan / Progressive Relaxation Meditation

Now that you know the way to go about different meditation postures, you are ready to know about the various types of meditation. There are various types of meditation such as Zen Meditation, Spiritual meditation, Mantra meditation among others. In this chapter, we will extensively discuss body scan/progressive relaxation meditation.

What is Body Scan Meditation?

When you hear "body scan", you can be forgiven to think that it involves the use of a machine to scan your body while meditating. However, surprisingly, body scan meditation is not that sophisticated. It is possible that you don't pay attention to the physical comfort you are experiencing in your body such as tense muscles, headache, shoulder and back pain as a result of the level of stress you are experiencing. Most times, these physical discomforts are linked to the state of your emotions.

The state of your mind can affect the way you feel physically. You can feel so alive and full of vitality when you have the right state of mind and you can have physical issues because of what goes on in your mind. Body scan meditation aims at helping you release the tension you may not even realize you are going through. This meditation involves focusing on parts of your body and the accompanying sensations. It is a gradual process in which you pay attention to your body parts from your head to your feet. It is a mental process in which you scan and bring yourself into the awareness of what is happening to your body.

This meditation will help you notice sensations such as tension, pains, aches, and any other general discomfort in your body. Body scan meditation does not make these negative sensations disappear; it will help you learn about them to the end that you will be able to manage them better. You can carry out this meditation either daily or even several times a day depending on your schedule and determination.

Benefits of Body Scan Meditation

There are many benefits you stand to enjoy from the practice of body scan meditation:

Release of Tension

This type of meditation is an effective remedy for stress and tension. You will find yourself being able to remain in a calm state as you let go of tension easily with this meditation.

Reduction of Inflammation, Insomnia, and Fatigue

Body scan meditation does not only help you release tension. There are other benefits to this type of meditation with scientific evidence. The practice of body scan meditation regularly helps to reduce inflammation, insomnia, and fatigue. According to research carried out by Woods-Giscombé and his colleagues in 2014 on "The Cultural Relevance of Mindfulness Meditation as a Health Intervention for African Americans: Implications for Reducing Stress-Related Health Disparities", meditation reduces stress which in turn leads to the reduction of inflammation, insomnia, and fatigue. Via body scan meditation, the cycle of physical and psychological tension is broken. Hence, you will be able to stay calm and relaxed with ease with the regular practice of body scan meditation.

Enjoy Every Moment

With body scan meditation, you will be able to subject your mind to enjoy the moment rather than be anxious and tensed. You will no longer go through life passively. You will be able to stop your monkey mind from being too restless and going wild. You will be able to train your mind to explore both pleasant and unpleasant sensations and learn from them. It enables you to travel through your body without the need to change or fix anything. You are like a visitor in your own body checking through the sensations and taking notes for future use.

How to Practice Body Scan/Progressive Relaxation Meditation

Now that you know the benefit of body scan meditation, it is time to know how to practice it. Just like other forms of meditation, body scan meditation is not difficult to practice. Below are some things that will enable you to be effective in the practice of this form of meditation

Ensure you are Comfortable

The most important thing in the practice of any form of meditation is to be comfortable. Meditation is to bring you comfort at the end of the day. Hence, if you start out uncomfortable, you are already setting up yourself to be frustrated in the long run. Comfort begins from the posture of your body and extends to your outfit. Just as I have mentioned in the previous chapter, you can practice meditation by sitting, kneeling, lying down, and standing. What matters is to find a posture that best makes you comfortable. It is not a crime to try different postures until you discover the one that is best for you.

As regards the outfit also, I have explained in the previous chapter that you should not wear tight-fitted clothing for maximum concentration. As much as you should be modest especially when you are practicing meditation in a public place, you should never sacrifice it for comfort. Hence, it is better you practice body scan meditation at home where you can be comfortable rather than go somewhere you will be restricted. It is always good to practice where there are other people to encourage you. However, always ensure you are comfortable.

Take a Few Deep Breaths

Slow down your breathing deliberately when practicing this form of meditation. Avoid breathing from your chest but from your belly. It is easier to control the pace of your breathing when you breathe from your belly. Let your abdomen expand and contract with every breath. If you notice that your shoulder is falling and rising, it shows that you are not yet breathing from your belly. Put the focus on breathing from your belly. When you are doing it correctly, your belly will move as though it is a balloon inflating and deflating rhythmically.

There are breathing exercises that can help you practice body scan meditation effectively. For example, you can go for "mindful diaphragmic breathing". This breathing exercise involves closing your eyes and start noticing your breath while you are in a comfortable position. Notice the pace and depth to see whether it is shallow or deep. This will help you become aware of your breathing pattern and relax more when necessary.

You can also consider counted breathing exercises. This breathing exercise involves placing your tongue on the roof of your mouth behind your teeth while inhaling through your nose. While breathing, slowly count from 1 to 5 before you exhale. This breathing exercise will help you control the pace of your breath and stretch your exhalation.

Bring Awareness to Your Feet

While breathing, slowly bring your attention to your feet. Start to observe the sensations in your feet. In case you observe the pain, notice it and also any emotions or thoughts that come with it. Don't increase the pace of your breathing as a result of this action. Slowly breathe as you observe these sensations, thoughts, and emotions.

Focus and Breath into the Tension

In case you observe any sensations that are not comfortable, don't ignore them. Focus on these sensations and breathe into them to notice the reactions. Imagine the tension leaving your body as you breathe. Visualize the tensions evaporating away into the air. When you feel you are ready for the next phase, move on. Remember that meditation is more about the mind rather than physical experiences.

Hence, it is vital that you can visualize your tensions disappearing as you practice meditation. Once you can handle the state of your mind, you are in the driving seat. This simple but powerful method will alleviate you of stress in a way that will amaze you. Hence, you won't see any physical mist or vapor going away but the mental process of visualization is enough to do the magic.

Entire Body Scan

The last phase of body scan meditation is the entire scanning of your body. You will do the same thing you did with your feet to the remaining parts of your body gradually. In other words, you will gently observe the sensations in the other parts of your body by starting with your feet upwards. You will not stop until you get to the top of your head. Observe how you are feeling and notice where you are holding stress. In case you feel any sensation like pain, tightness, or pressure, breathe into it. You will be able to ease any tension or stress this way and learn about it for future reference.

Other Important Tips

There are other important tips that will enable you to make the best out of body scan meditation. Here they are:Feel free to practice body scan meditation any time you feel stress. However, you don't have to feel stress before you practice body scan meditation. You don't always feel the physical comfort in your due to stress but you can always discover any discomfort through the practice of body scan meditation.

There is an abbreviated version of body scan meditation you can practice in case you don't have much time. It involves sitting and paying attention to any part of your body where you have tension instead of moving from your feet upward. It does not come off easily from the onset. Through regular practice of full body scan meditation, you will be able to pull off the abbreviated version with ease over time. However, don't get used to it because it is not as effective as the full body scan. You should only use it when you have a tight schedule and still want to stay healthy via meditation practice. The abbreviated version is not a shortcut but half bread which is better than none but not as good as full bread. Hence, schedule your time to practice body scan meditation at least 30 to 40 minutes daily. However, during days when you can't do that, all hope is not lost.

Chapter   Six: Loving-Kindness Meditation

We all want to be loved especially by people we care about the most. However, most people find it difficult to express love towards others. Loving-Kindness Meditation is a type of meditation that will help you find it easier in your heart to love others. You cannot love others if you have issues with accepting and loving yourself.

The word "Loving-Kindness" in Buddhism is "Maitri" which also means friendliness and benevolence. It is one of the ten paramis (perfections) of the Theravada school of Buddhism. In this chapter, you will learn about what loving-kindness meditation is all about, how to practice it, and the benefits you stand to enjoy by practicing it.

What is Loving-Kindness Meditation?

Loving-Kindness Meditation is a meditation practice that is popular for its ability to promote well-being and reduce stress. It is a self-care technique that enables to you living a healthy and happy life. Beyond physical health, Loving-Kindness Meditation helps you to walk in love and forgiveness towards people who hurt you. It also helps you to accept yourself and connect with others around you with ease.

In Loving-Kindness Meditation, while in a still position, you imagine someone who you respect or love stand by you while you meditate. The person may be someone in the present or someone in your past. As you meditate, you imagine the person standing on your right side sending you wishes for your health and prosperity. You will also do the same for your left side. This process of imagining people you love wishing you well is the foundation for receiving loving-kindness in this type of meditation.

You can also send your love and best wishes to people you love via this meditation. You do this by imagining yourself send the love you felt to the person on your left and right side. This meditation helps you to see how other people around you also need love just like you. Hence, your imagination of sending love to others will help your practice loving-kindness towards people around you more frequently.

Benefits of Practicing Loving-Kindness Meditation

Below are the benefits of practicing loving-kindness meditation:

Generation of Positive Energy

During loving-kindness meditation, you will be able to generate a lot of positive energy from loving yourself and others. People around you will start seeing you as a role model and an epitome of sacrifice when you practice this form of meditation.

Treatment of Borderline Personality

Apart from the feeling of relaxation and calmness you get from this meditation, there is more. A study carried out by Johannes Graser and Ulrich Stangier in 2018 reveals that loving-kindness meditation can be beneficial in the treatment of borderline personality and chronic pain. However, the study concluded that more evidences will be needed to support this claim.

How to Practice Loving-Kindness Meditation

There are various Buddhist traditions with different methods of practicing loving-kindness meditation. However, each of these methods has the same core psychological operation. The core principle of every method of practicing loving-kindness meditation is to generate affection towards some specific people in your life, yourself, as well as others. Below are some useful tips as regards the practice of loving-kindness meditation:

Set out Time to Practice

You cannot be too busy to pay attention to whatever matters to you. Whatever you don't have time for, you don't value. Hence, if it matters to you that you should increase the way you show love to people around you and yourself, you have to take out time to practice this type of meditation. You don't need so much time before you can engage in loving-kindness meditation. Just a few minutes are enough to do it. Once you are ready, find somewhere comfortable to sit. I don't have to repeat what I have said earlier about comfortable outfits. While your eyes are closed, relax your muscles, and take a few deep breaths to get started.

Visualization of Emotional and Physical Wellbeing

The next step is to visualize yourself experiencing total emotional and physical wellbeing and inner peace. Imagine yourself accepting yourself totally and loving yourself in an overwhelming way. Think of yourself as a person of worth and value and be grateful for who you are. Kick out every thought of words of ineptitude about your personality. See yourself as a person worth the love and affection of any reasonable person as you meditate. Feel the inner peace you get as you focus on these thoughts. As you inhale and exhale slowly, see it as you breathing in affection and breathing out tension and negative emotions.

Repeat Positive Phrases about Yourself

Don't just stop at thinking about yourself in a positive light and showering yourself with all the love in the world. You need to also say good things about yourself during meditation. Wish yourself well and pronounce positive words about your present and your future. Declare positive things about your health, finance, family, relationship, and other important areas of your life.

Say things like "I stay healthy", "My family is safe from all danger", "My finance is getting better" etc. You don't have to say these exact words. You can modify them according to your desire. What matters is to speak positive words about your life while in this relaxed and comfortable sitting position. Say these words slowly to avoid increasing the tempo of your breath and unsettling your previous equilibrium. Say these words at least three or four times.

Enjoy the Moment

Enjoy the moment as you bask in this moment of showering yourself with love and warmth. Don't let go of this precious moment quickly. Treasure the moment and enjoy the feeling of warmth and compassion towards yourself. Let these feelings of affection and compassion envelope you. It is possible that you find your attention drifting away to another though which may be neutral or contradictory. Don't fight it; just gently redirect your attention back to these thoughts of loving-kindness. Take your time and let the feeling overwhelm you. Focus on yourself completely in this phase before you move on to the next phase.

Focus on Others

After focusing on the feeling of compassion for yourself, the next phase is to focus on other people in your life. You can start with someone very close and dear to you first like your child or your spouse. Feel your love and appreciation for the person as you meditate. Think about how much the person means to you and let the feeling of compassion and affection for the person overwhelm you for a while. Speak the same or similar positive words you spoke about yourself earlier about the person too. Of course, that will imply that you will change the "Is" to "you". Just speak freely about the health and progress of the person as you shower compassion on the person.

One after the Other

After holding the feeling of compassion for the first person for a while, move on to another person who is important to you. Imagine every one of them living happily in good health and having inner peace. Bring in your friends before moving on to your family members, neighbors, and colleagues. The people you focus on does not necessarily have to be people who are living close to you alone. You can extend this loving-kindness to people across the globe. You can spare a thought for people struggling with terminal diseases, malnutrition, and extreme poverty all over the world. Wish them well and feel your compassion towards them. Connect with them and have empathy towards them.

However, the height of this phase is when you focus on people who have hurt you in the past or recently. Shower your compassion on them too and experience tremendous inner peace. It is easy to love people who care about you but it is difficult to have compassion for people who don't wish you well. If you can push yourself to extend your feeling of compassion towards them and wish them well, the inner peace you will feel is immeasurable.

Internalize the Experience

After you are done with the meditation, open your eyes and relish the wonderful journey. You can think about the inner peace and nice sensation you felt during the meditation all day long. Remember the inner peace you enjoyed to remind you to practice loving-kindness towards yourself and other people in your life. Internalize the feeling so that it will spur you to practice it again some other time. Take a few deep breaths before you finally bring the meditation to an end.

Other Important Tips

Other important tips that will help you get the best out of loving-kindness meditation include:

As a beginner, focus on only yourself when meditating. In other words, perfect your ability to imagine the feeling of compassion and speaking positive words with yourself as the sole subject. You will be able to bring in others later when you are comfortable with practicing with yourself first.

Bring in people you find difficult to forgive last. You may not have enough inner strength to genuinely forgive such people until you have practiced loving-kindness towards yourself and the people you love first. Forgiveness is not complete until you can both imagine the offender doing well and speaking positive phrases about the wellbeing of such a person.

Set an alarm if you want to avoid spending too much time practicing this meditation. However, you don't need an alarm as a beginner. The need for an alarm should arise after you have practiced such that you have reaped the benefits consistently.

The above method is not the only way to practice loving-kindness meditation. This is just a sample which you can modify slightly or drastically to suit your need. However, the principle of relaxation and feeling compassion towards yourself and other people remains constant. You can alter other procedures but not these two.

Chapter Seven: Spiritual Meditation

Spiritual meditation is all about knowing yourself the way you are and not based on inaccurate perceptions you had about yourself. It is important to note that different religions such as Hinduism, Buddhism, Daoism, and Christian faith all practice spiritual meditation. In this chapter, you will be introduced to spiritual meditation, its benefits, and practices.

Meditation in Hinduism, Buddhism, Daoism, and Christian Faith

Meditation in Hinduism is an important practice. Meditation in Hinduism is carried out to achieve oneness between the non-dual almighty (Brahman) and the spirit of the practitioner. This state of oneness is called Moksha. In the Hindu scriptures, there were monks who attained supernatural power through the practice of meditation.

Meditation in Buddhism is similar to Hinduism. Historians believe that the practice of meditation was passed from Hinduism to Buddhism as Buddha; the founder of Buddhism was a Hindu. The difference is that meditation in Hinduism has different purposes and ultimately to connect with God. However, Buddhists don't believe in God but see meditation as an integral part of their religion.

Meditation in Daoism is similar to Buddhism. Some techniques used in Daoism were developed from mindfulness practices in Buddhism. Meditation in the Christian faith involves thinking about the scriptures to obtain revelation from God. Do you need to have a religion you practice before you can practice spiritual meditation? No.

What is Spiritual Meditation?

Spiritual meditation is a type of meditation that connects you with your real self. It involves stripping yourself of your perceptions as you delve into a peaceful and still state of mind. This type of meditation involves sitting in a calm manner while clearing your mind and enjoying the moment. It involves deep breaths, visualizing, uttering a prayer, and even humming. Spiritual meditation is not restrictive and you can always modify it to what suits your needs.

Don't assume that spiritual meditation means that you have to be religious. It is true that different religions practice spiritual meditation but you don't have to be religious to practice it. It is all about connecting to something greater and deeper than you. It involves honest self-reflection to increase your level of spiritual awareness. It requires an attitude of integrity and genuineness while looking at yourself and the world.

As your spiritual confidence and awareness increase, you will be able to live a life that will be beneficial to others. Whether you know it or not, you have been on a spiritual journey since you became conscious as a person. Although the journey to spiritual enlightenment takes time, the benefits are worthwhile. Spiritual meditation is not a quick fix to all your problems but a journey of self-evaluation and reflection. For people who place a premium on their spiritual growth (we all should), spiritual meditation is non-negotiable.

Benefits of Spiritual Meditation

There are emotional, cognitive, mental, and physical benefits that come with the practice of spiritual meditation. Below are the benefits of practicing spiritual meditation:

Reduction of Stress and Anxiety

Just like other forms of meditation, spiritual meditation helps in the reduction of stress and anxiety. Spiritual meditation is a short-term and long-term remedy for mental stress and anxiety. Blacks and his colleagues in 2015 discovered in their research that consistent practice of meditation decreases stress and anxiety.

Happiness and Meaning

This form of meditation is also able to make your experience as a person better. It has proven to make people a happy and meaningful life. According to the EOC Institute, there are seven main neurotransmitters that are involved during spiritual meditation. The hormones responsible for happiness, serotonin and endorphin are released during the practice of spiritual meditation. There is a change of mood that occurs during this meditation that will affect your overall happiness in the short and long run.

Enhanced Memory

The EOC Institute also reckons that spiritual meditation can bring about enhanced memory in the long run.

Immunity

Spiritual meditation also improves your immunity against both common and fatal diseases. According to a study carried out by David Black and George Slavich in 2016, the result showed that meditation can bring about a reduction of proinflammatory processes. The study also revealed that meditation can lead to an increase in enzyme activity and cell-mediated defense parameters.

Reduction of Physical Pain

According to the Cleveland Clinic, the practice of spiritual meditation helps you to reduce physical pain. The practice of spiritual meditation helps you to focus on other things apart from the pain thereby leading to a reduction in the pain you feel.

Control Negative Emotions and Increase Life Span

Spiritual meditation can also help you control negative emotions and increase your life span according to the EOC Institute.

How to Practice Spiritual Meditation

It is simple and straightforward to practice spiritual meditation. Below are the steps to follow:

Get a Calm Place to Sit

The foundation of every form of meditation is to find a peaceful place you can practice it and spiritual meditation is not different. This meditation just like other types of meditation requires concentration and a peaceful place where you can be alone with your thought is very vital. Some people are still able to concentrate even in a place with minimal distraction but it is always better to find a serene environment for maximal concentration. After finding the perfect place for you, sit down and concentrate and shut out every form of distraction.

Close Your Eyes

The level of concentration required in spiritual meditation requires that you close your eyes. It is especially important that you close your eyes all through the duration of the meditation if you are just getting to start this form of meditation. When your eyes are open, it is easy for you to pay attention to a stimulus in the environment that will prevent you from totally submerging into a state of meditation. It is not easy for whatever you are not seeing to distract you. Hence, to submerge yourself into a complete state of meditation, it is better you close your eyes.

Be in Charge of Your Thoughts

After closing your eyes, you need to take charge of your thoughts by keeping it quiet. Your thoughts don't make any audible sound to others but they can be the loudest for you. Hence, you need to avoid being distracted by those lousy and cluttered thoughts. Take your time to clear your mind as you get set to surge into a full meditative state.

You need a relaxed state of mind to get the best out of spiritual meditation. It is in the midst of a quiet mind that you can connect with your through and higher self. Remember that the end of spiritual meditation is to strip off wrong impressions and see yourself in the true light. Hence, you need a clear state of mind to achieve this and not pick the wrong perception.

Let Go of Any Grudges

You cannot submerge into a complete meditative state when you have grudges against people. Sometimes, you hold grudges subconsciously and that is why you should do a little bit of soul-searching. Forgiveness is a critical part of spiritual meditation. It is impossible to get the full experience of spiritual meditation when you still have painful grudges in your heart. Let go of disappointments and betrayals by people around you. Meditation is meant to also help you feel compassion towards people in your life. Hence, you will be starting on a wrong note when you are hurting and don't want to let go.

Be Open-minded

You will learn a lot through the practice of spiritual meditation and that is why it is important you keep an open mind. You will grow and get better as a person through this experience and you must be ready to learn. You have to mentally take yourself outside your comfort zone. This is done by forgiving yourself and also people in your life. Let go of negative emotions and your regular thought pattern. This journey of discovering yourself needs you to keep an open mind to get the best out of it.

Pay Attention to Your Breath

You breathe all day long but you don't pay attention to your pattern of breathing most times. In the practice of spiritual meditation, you need to focus on your breathing. Observe the depth of each breath and the movement of your body as you inhale and exhale. Also, observe how long you hold your breath. This breathing exercise will not only help you breathe properly but calm your chattering mind.

Visualization and Muttering

The last phase of spiritual meditation involves visualizing yourself in a serene environment. You can imagine a bright white light touching your head and cleansing your soul of childhood hurt and other grievances. To feel that inner peace en route to self-discovery, speak words that carry positive energy about you. Speak about your health and other areas of your life. Take note of the phrases you spoke that made you feel better the most. Use those phrases often any time you meditate.

Other Important Tips

If you are new to spiritual meditation, it is not an issue. As long as you keep an open mind and a willingness to learn, you will be fine. Below are important tips that can help your practice spiritual meditation effectively:

Ensure you are comfortable both in your sitting position and your outfit. The importance of comfort when it comes to spiritual meditation cannot be overemphasized. It is the foundation of your journey to connecting with your true self.

Make sure your body is in a relaxed state before and during meditation. If you notice that your body is not relaxed, you can deliberately tense up your muscles and relax them as you breathe slowly.

If you find it difficult to keep a quiet mind during meditation, you can hum a favorite tune. Breathe slowly and feel the ambience of a peaceful mind.

Don't be perturbed about how well you are doing but the experience itself. In other words, don't get anxious about whether you are practicing meditation correctly or not. You should get more knowledge before or after the meditation. However, while practicing, the only thing that should be on your mind is the experience of connecting with your higher self and not how well you are doing it.

Don't restrict yourself to any particular environment. You can experiment with both indoor and outdoor meditation. You cannot know what is best for you until you try different options.

Never stop learning about how to improve your meditation practice. Get books and any other material that will help your experience. If you can get a teacher you can trust to teach you one-on-one, it is also a good option. You can take meditation classes also to get better.

If you stop practicing spiritual meditation, you may lose the previous experience. Hence, just like exercises and sports, you need regular practice. A daily habit of practicing meditation will do you a whole lot of good. It is fun and helpful. So, why not daily?

You can set reminders on your phone every day to remind you to practice every day. You can also get friends and family to practice with you so that you can encourage yourselves to practice daily.

Chapter Eight: Focused Meditation

Every form of meditation requires you to focus on it. Hence, focused meditation cannot be all about maintaining your focus any time you meditate. Focus is one of the most important things you can have in life. What you focus on is where you place your attention. Meanwhile, your attention is what determines the direction of your life. You drive, passion, and commitment is towards whatever is the focal point of your life.

What is Focused Meditation?

Focused meditation is a type of meditation in which you focus on a particular moment before moving on to another moment while meditating. It is a popular Buddhist practice where you learn to sustain your attention on selective moments to experience inner peace and release tension. What to focus on during this meditation can be something external. This form of meditation is not rigid. It allows you to bring in external influences to help focus your attention. You can focus on the sound of a gong or just staring at a candle flame. You can also use mala beads and just concentrate on counting them.

Any of your five senses can be used to concentrate during this meditation. This form of meditation helps you to measure the quality of your ability to pay attention to something. As you try to focus on your breath or any other thing of choice, you can find your mind moving to the pain you are feeling in a part of your leg. You may also find your attention drifting to something unpleasant that took place at your workplace or between you and your spouse.

You let go of the distraction and return your mind to the chosen focal point. Basically, you are training your mind to focus more on a selective thing and not wander about during this meditation. The particular thing you are focusing on is your anchor and you will know when you have moved away from it. You will learn from this drifting and bring your mind back to where it ought to be.

Benefits of Practicing Focused Meditation

The practice of focused meditation is fun but also beneficial. Below are some benefits of practicing meditation:

Recognition of Distractions

When you practice focused meditation, you will be able to develop a monitoring awareness that enables you to detect distractions. You cannot know what distracts you unless you have a specific focus. Hence, whatever drifts your attention away from your initial focal point will be labeled as a distraction. This will enable you to detect distractions in your life in your daily life. You will learn to set clearly defined goals and notice when something else is taking away your attention from your goal.

Ability to Disengage from Distractions

During focused meditation, you will learn to disengage from distractions while meditating. Therefore, you will not only learn to recognize distractions but also disengage from them when you practice focused meditation. This will result in you being able to disengage yourself from distractions in your daily activity.

Ability to Refocus

It is not just good enough to recognize and disengage from distractions; you must be able to refocus your attention again on the selected focal point. The practice of focused meditation trains your mind to bring your attention back to where it was before it drifted away. It is actually fun to practice this form of meditation. It feels like playing a racing game where you are racing against the tides. You are holding on to the "steering wheel" of your mind and bringing it back to where the tides have moved it away.

More Productivity

Your performance and productivity are impaired when you are distracted. Once you learn to recognize and disengage from distractions via this meditation, your performance in your daily activities will definitely get better. You will know when something else is taking your attention away from your job, family, or loved ones. You will disengage on time and be better in your career and the way you handle your relationships with others.

How to Practice Focused Meditation

You can become a pro in the practice of focused meditation in no time. Here are some tips that can help you:

Set out Time for Practice

It is always important you decide how long you want to practice to maintain consistency. You can go for 15 minutes daily or 4 times a day. You can do more but just be consistent. As long as you are consistent, you are good to go.

Find a comfortable Place to Practice

If I have to say this a thousand times, it is worth it. Every form of meditation demands that you practice in the correct environment. You cannot focus when you have sounds blaring and people distracting you. Hence, it is vital that you find somewhere with little or no distraction. You don't have to find a place where there is perfect silence as that will make a graveyard the only perfect place to practice.

Decide Your Focus

After finding a place to practice, the next step is to decide what will be your focal point. It is totally your choice to decide what you will use as an anchor for your thought. It can be the sound of a metronome or a nice picture. As long as the stimulus is good enough to stimulate you, you are good to go. You don't have to use what other people use. Focused meditation allows you to be creative with your choice of an anchor.

Get into a Comfortable Position

What you need next is to get into a meditation position that suits you. Relax your body and loosen your shoulder. Breathe slowly from your belly as against your chest to control the pace of your breath. Most people who practice focused meditation cross their legs but you don't have to do that. If you are comfortable with crossing your legs, it is good. However, if you find another position that is more comfortable for you, go for it. Your meditation position should not be such that it makes you sleep. Be active but relaxed when meditating.

Focus on the Chosen Target

Once you are in a comfortable position, focus on the target you have previously selected. Just like a hitman, set your radar on that sound, smell, or image you have made your focal point. Savor every detail and analyze it. The idea of focusing on a target is not to just pay attention to it but to experience it. If it is a sound, notice the tempo, think about how different it could have been. If it is a picture, observe every line and color combination. Let every detail come alive to you. Be fully present and enjoy the moment.

Calm Your Inner Voice

Your chattering mind will try to prevent you from enjoying the moment. The same way you find yourself drifting from a particular thing in your daily life is what also takes place during the meditation. Learn to master the art of bringing calm to your monkey mind during this meditation and translate it to your day-to-day activity. Your inner voice will remind you about something else but you have to gently return your attention to the focal point. It is during this process that you learn to recognize distractions, disengage from them, and refocus again. Learn from the drifting pattern and use it as a template in practical daily activities.

Don't be concerned about Failing

The common pitfall people who practice various forms of meditation including focused meditation fall into is evaluating their success while meditating. Thinking about whether you are doing it right or wrong in itself is a distraction. You have succeeded in taking your mind away from the chosen target to another thought. Therefore, always evaluate yourself after meditation and not while meditating. There is always room for improvement and you should seek to get better. However, you are not doing yourself any good when you allow the thought of doing it correctly or not distract you from focusing on the chosen target.

Other Important Tips

There are other things you need to know that can help you practice focused meditation more effectively. The steps above are to guide you and serve as a template but there is room for modification. You may struggle initially with each step. Below are important tips that can make your practice easier:

Don't be in a hurry to be perfect. It takes practice to practice focused meditation perfectly. It is not difficult but you need to give it time. Giving it time does not mean that you should not practice; it means that you should practice patiently. Celebrate every progress; don't be too critical of yourself. Enjoy the journey and the learning process.

You don't have to start with fifteen minutes. You can start with shorter sessions like 5 minutes as a starter. Patiently increase the time you spend as you get better. There is no in point spending time when you are not effective. Ease yourself into the practice and build your effectiveness over time.

If you are finding it difficult to handle focused meditation, you don't have to quit meditating altogether. You can try other forms of meditating first and try focused meditation later. Every form of meditation has the same basics. Hence, if you are able to "crack the code" with another form of meditation, you can find it easier with focused meditation.

Don't follow stereotypes. For some people, the best time for them to meditate is early in the morning while some people find joy meditating in the cool of the evening. Some people are even comfortable with both. Find the best time for you to practice. Don't just copy what other people do because the fact that it worked for them does not mean it will work for you.

Chapter Nine: Zen Meditation

Zen is a Japanese term that has the same meaning as the Chinese word "Ch'an" and Indian word "dhyana" all meaning meditation or concentration. Zen meditation is also called "zazen" and it is a type of meditation built upon Buddhist psychology and traditions. It is an interesting form of meditation with myriads of benefits. In this chapter, you will learn what Zen meditation is all about and how you can practice it.

What is Zen Meditation?

Zen meditation is often described as a meditation that helps you to "think about not thinking". This description is not far from the truth about Zen meditation. This form of meditation involves looking within and gaining awareness and focus. Unlike focused meditation, it does not involve focusing on any particular target. However, just like focused meditation, Zen meditation enables you to train your monitoring skills.

This monitoring without a specific target is the reason Zen meditation is often described as an "open-monitoring meditation". It does not involve the recitation of any mantra or cultivation of compassion like loving-kindness meditation but there is still a lot of focus on self-awareness. Unlike any other form of meditation, the eyes are kept semi-open in Zen meditation. The target of your attention during the practice of Zen meditation is nothing!

In other words, during Zen meditation, you are not thinking about anything in particular and that is why it is described as a meditation where you think about not thinking. All you do is to fight off any thought that tries to pop into your mind while you are in a calm and relaxed state. The idea of this meditation is to help you tap into your subconscious mind. You will be able to detect preconceived notions and discover your thought pattern and insight into yourself.

Benefits of Practicing Zen Meditation

Just like other forms of meditation, Zen meditation has many benefits. It offers calmness and helps you to release tension just like other types of meditation but much more. There are psychological, physical, cognitive, and spiritual benefits you can derive from this form of meditation. You can enjoy the following when you practice Zen meditation regularly:

Insight into the Nature of your Body and Mind

The regular practice of Zen meditation will help you gain insight into how your mind works. You will also be able to learn about some of your reflex actions. You will be able to shutout mainstream thoughts and learn about your thought pattern.

Enhanced Focus

The interest of scientists to understand how meditation affects the body and mind has led to some researches with interesting results. In 2008, Giuseppe Pagnoni, Milos Cekic, and Ying Guo carried out research on the correlates of conceptual processing during Zen Meditation. Ten Zen practitioners who all have more than three years of daily practice were used in this study.

The result of the study showed that there are activities in the brain "default network" regions. These regions of the brain are linked to wandering minds. This result shows that the regular practice of Zen meditation can enhance your focus and ability to pay attention to specific things.

Limitation of Distraction

The enhanced focus will translate to the ability to keep out distractions. Focus and keeping out distractions are difficult to achieve in the digital world we have today. So much time is spent on gadgets, mobile phones, and computers in the modern world. Therefore, the ability to maintain your focus and avoid distraction is very vital.

Access to the Unconscious Mind

Zen meditation makes it possible for you to access your unconscious mind. This claim has raised some dust but it is true and supported by scientific evidence. Does it really matter that you gain access to your unconscious mind? Yes! Why? Your conscious mind can only focus on one thing at a time but your unconscious mind can do more than that. Therefore access to your unconscious mind can unlock a higher level of creativity and performance.

In 2012, a study was carried out to examine the possibility of gaining access to your unconscious mind via the practice of Zen meditation. The participants were all seasoned Zen practitioners. A group was asked to read magazines while the other group was asked to meditate for 20 minutes. The two groups were then asked to solve a puzzle on the computer screen. The people who meditated were able to solve the puzzle faster than those who read magazines. The result of this study shows that Zen meditation enables you to access your unconscious mind.

Treatment of Drug Abuse

Most forms of meditation lead to a connection between the mind and the body. However, Zen meditation takes it a notch higher as it causes an interaction between the heart and the brain! A study in 2018 carried out by Lo Pei-Chen and other scientists was able to establish this interaction. According to this study, Zen meditation makes it possible to connect with the spiritual heart which is located in the organ heart.

The authors of this study reckoned that years of Zen meditation practice helps the practitioners to have their brain in such a way that it is dominated by the spiritual heart. It is this heart and brain interaction that makes it possible to treat drug addiction with regular Zen meditation. Zen meditation serves as the foundation of drug abuse treatment programs in Taiwan. This type of meditation affects the autonomous nervous system which is the system that is responsible for bodily functions such as breathing, digestive processes, and heartbeat.

People suffering from drug abuse often have issues with their autonomous system during their recovery. Zen meditation improves mood and people recovering from drug addiction needs an improved mood to prevent them from abusing drugs again.

How to Practice Zen Meditation

You don't have to find a monk before you can practice Zen meditation. Below are steps you can follow to practice this form of meditation:

Sit in a Relaxing Place

You need a place devoid of distractions to practice Zen meditation. It may be indoors or outdoors as long as you can meditate there without distractions, it is fine. You can create a special atmosphere if you are meditating indoors by creating an altar. You can make the altar with items like flowers, seashells, and stones. Lighting a candle can also help you create a serene and spiritual atmosphere to meditate.

Get into a Stable Position

The way you seat is crucial in Zen meditation. Hence, ensure you are sitting comfortably such that you keep your back straight. You can cross your legs or support yourself with a pillow to ensure that you are comfortable and ready for meditation.

Position Your Head Correctly

The way you position your head is also important in this form of meditation. Let your head be in a position that is natural such that you don't strain your body. Let your spine align with your neck as though a straight line is running up your spine to your neck.

Relax the Muscles of Your Jaw and Face

It is important that you don't strain your body when meditating. Hence, ensure you relax your jaw and facial muscles. Before you start meditating, notice if there is any tension in the jaw or facial muscles and release them.

Breathe Through Your Nose

There is a lot of focus on breathing in the practice of Zen meditation. You need to breathe through your nose and feel the cooling and warmth sensation produced via your inhalation and exhalation. Nasal breathes will enable you to monitor the rhythm of your breath all through the meditation.

Pay Attention to your Breath

You have to focus on your breath when you start meditating as much as you can. Focus on the rhythm and sound of your breath as you inhale and exhale. Feel the warmth and cooling sensations as air passes in and out of your lungs. You will pay attention to your breath not just at the beginning of the meditation but all through the meditation.

Decide on what to do with your Eyes

Many people keep their eyes closed when practicing Zen meditation. However, there is no harm in keeping them open or semi-open. However, if you are keeping your eyes open, you need to focus on a particular point in the room. What matters is that you feel natural, comfortable, and not distracted.

Be in Charge of your Mind

Your mind will wander because you are sitting in silence but you have to be in charge. Your mind can go to other things you need to do later in the day or the mistakes you made in the past. There is no limit to what your mind can ponder about. However, you have to gently redirect it back to your breath all through the meditation. Your mind may even drift to thinking about whether you are carrying out the meditation correctly. However, you have to be in charge of your mind and not let it wander.

Other Important Tips

Apart from the basics, the following information should be beneficial to you:

If you are struggling with the alignment of your neck and spine, tuck in your chin.

Use your fingers to massage your jaws slightly if you notice that your jaw feels tense to loosen up the muscles of your face.

Struggle with keeping your mind quiet in the early stage of practice is not an anomaly. Don't be discouraged because you will get better with regular practice over time.

Avoid meditating for long as a starter. You may struggle to focus on your breath if you meditate for long as a beginner.

Hence, start by meditating for two minutes and improve on it with practice.

You can buy a small or zafu pillow to make your practice more effective. A zafu pillow is designed specifically for Zen meditation and you will do well to get one.

Just like other forms of meditation, don't be perturbed about perfection from the onset. Be excited and contented about the fact that you were able to start. Enjoy the experience and learn from your mistakes as you seek to get better.

Chapter Ten: Mantra Meditation

The words you speak reflect the state of your mind. You cannot know a person who is pessimistic by just looking at the face of the person. You will know a pessimist by the words spoken by the person. In the same way, you can only know an optimist when the person speaks. In the same way, you can change the state of your mind by speaking the right words. Mantra meditation is a form of meditation that takes advantage of speaking positive words. This chapter is a compendium of important things you need to know about this type of meditation, its practice, and its benefits.

What is Mantra Meditation?

Mantra meditation, just like most forms of meditation has Hindu and Buddhist roots. However, recitation of sacred words is also a tradition found in Judeo-Christianity as well. However, in recent times, the practice of mantra meditation is becoming more popular in non-religious mindfulness practice. A mantra refers to a word, syllable, or phrase that is spoken repeatedly during meditation. You don't have to speak audibly before it can be called a mantra. You may whisper it, chant it, or just repeat it in your mind.

It is important to note that it is not any word or syllable you chant that is a mantra. It is the energy associated with the muttering or chanting that produces the powerful effect that makes it a mantra. During meditation, mantra serves as an anchor point for a wandering mind. In other words, mantra meditation involves chanting or thinking about a set of words or syllables to train your mind to focus and experience the moment. You should know the meaning of the mantra to make the practice more effective. A mantra can be something like "I have much to celebrate" or "I am kind to myself".

There are various reasons people practice mantra meditation. For some people, they practice it to protect themselves against negative emotions. For other people, it is what they do to improve their sleep. However, in both Christian and Hindu tradition, mantra meditation recitation has a spiritual purpose. It is practiced to gain connection and intimacy with the divine. However, it is different in Buddhism because of the lack of belief in God. In Buddhism, mantra meditation aids focus and enjoyment of the present moment.

Benefits of Practicing Mantra Meditation

Mantra meditation is not without benefits and that is why a lot of people practice it regularly. According to the Eco Institute, below are benefits of practicing mantra meditation regularly:

Improvement of the Brain Functions

The regular practice of mantra meditation improves 9 key regions in the brain. The result of this improvement is that your stress level will reduce and you will also find it easier to sleep. Other benefits of this improvement include enhanced memory, ease of learning, higher EQ & IQ as well as more happiness.

Increased Life Span

Regular mantra meditation makes people who practice it look younger and live longer. According to the Eco Institute, mantra meditation boosts glutathione (GSH) which is an antioxidant. Glutathione is the most important antioxidant in the body. People who have terminal diseases like cancer or AIDS usually have their level of glutathione depleted. Glutathione is important for the maintenance of intracellular health. Hence, don't be surprised to know that regular mantra meditation can make you look way younger than your age and increase your life expectancy.

Prevention of Weight Loss

Stress can lead to an increase in heart rate and the tension can become unbearable when it is intense. One of the results of intense stress levels is the loss of weight. When you practice mantra meditation regularly, you will be able to keep your mind quiet and reduce your stress level. Indirectly, you are preventing yourself from suffering the loss of weight.

Access to your Subconscious and Unconscious Mind

Your subconscious and unconscious minds contain the requisite creative solution you need to take your life a notch higher. You will have a little taste of what lies within when you are half-awake early in the morning. You find great ideas come into your mind and you begin to wonder why you have never thought about them before. Where did these wonderful ideas come from? Your subconscious and unconscious mind! Imagine how much you will be able to do when you can expressly access your subconscious and unconscious mind! Thankfully, consistent practice of mantra meditation is the key that gives you access to your subconscious and unconscious mind.

Boost of Brain Chemicals

Key brain chemicals such as Endorphins, GABA, and Serotonin are boosted through the practice of mantra meditation. Cortisol is the hormone in the body linked to stress. In 2013, Turakitwanakan and his colleagues studied the effects of mindfulness meditation on serum Cortisol of medical students. The result of the research revealed that mindfulness meditation decreases the Cortisol levels in the blood thereby reducing stress and preventing psychiatric disorder.

Improved Immune System

The practice of this form of meditation boosts your immune system. Consistent mantra meditation is more like training your body to act like a fully loaded Mack truck to crush germs that comes against it. Your body has "soldiers" that protect it against germs and these soldiers are "T cells" and "antibodies". When you practice mantra meditation regularly, these warriors are boosted and help your body to fight against diseases without you even knowing about it.

Fight against Addiction

The brain "happiness center", the prefrontal cortex, is activated when you practice mantra meditation regularly. The implication of this activation is that you will have a "natural high" which ensures that you don't need to depend on any drug. Therefore, you will never have any reason to deal with addiction.

Development of Willpower

Willpower is important for success in the future. It takes willpower to have confidence in your ability to work hard and achieve your goals in life. Willpower is never automatic; it is developed by training and practice. The kind of training of the mind you get through mantra meditation develops your willpower and set you up for success in the future. Top executives are beginning to understand this benefit and they are practicing meditation more than ever in recent times.

How to Practice Mantra Meditation

By now, you already know that you need to get a serene environment to practice no matter the form of meditation you prefer. Regardless of your purpose for practicing mantra meditation; the following steps will help you:

Decide the Purpose of the Meditation

The reason for your practice of mantra meditation is what will determine the mantra you will use. Hence, you need to settle on whether you want to practice this form of meditation for the health benefit it offers or to achieve spiritual connection. Once you decide the purpose of the meditation, you are ready for the next step.

Get an appropriate Mantra for your Purpose of Meditation

Don't let this step bother you because there are already universal mantras you can use that supports your intention. The right mantra creates vibrations that resonate with your purpose. Every mantra has its own energy and you need to find the mantra whose vibration corresponds with your purpose for meditation. Regardless of your purpose, you can chant the universal mantra, "aum" repeatedly. It creates such a powerful vibration in your lower abdomen that makes you want to do it again. For peace of mind, you can chant "Hare Krishna, Hare Krishna, Krishna Krishna, Hare Hare, Hare Rama, Hare Rama, Rama Rama, Hare, Hare".

Sit Appropriately

The ideal sitting position for this form of meditation is sitting comfortably such that you cross your legs and your hips are elevated. This sitting position will help you align your spine with your neck in a straight way. In this sitting position, close your eyes for maximum concentration.

Focus on your Breathe

Focus on your breath but avoid the temptation to try to control it. Focus on the feeling of warmth and cooling sensation while exhaling and inhaling. The essence of this breathing exercise is to keep you relaxed in a meditative state.

Chant your Chosen Mantra

Having gain mastery over your breath, you are ready to chant your chosen mantra. There is no particular way to chant your chosen mantra. Chanting mantra is so powerful that you will get a lot of benefits from a small amount of chanting. You should also decide whether you want to continue to chant silently in your mind or audibly. It is not good to drift from audible chanting to mindfulness. You need focus and stability and that is why you should make up your mind on time. Stick with one because anyone you choose will be beneficial to you.

Meditate until you are Satisfied

There is no limitation to the time you can meditate. However, the longer you meditate the better for you. Just like sports, an athlete who practices longer and consistently will be fit and record better performance than a sloppy athlete. In the same way, the more you practice meditation, the more you will reap the benefits. It is only by practice, dedication, and commitment that you can move from being a naïve practitioner to an expert who can train others.

Other Important Tips

Other helpful tips you need to enjoy the practice of mantra meditation include:

Controlling your breath is not that easy and you should not be discouraged if you struggle initially. You will get better with time as you continue to practice.

If you find it difficult to meditate while sitting, you can use a chair and you can even do it while lying down.

If you don't want to use "aum" or any other mantra because you are not familiar with them, you can chant words that you know. As long as the words resonate with your purpose, you are doing well.

The best time to practice mantra meditation is early in the morning before your mind is encumbered by other thoughts. However, if you are not able to do it in the morning, do it at other periods of the day. The most important thing is regular practice because consistency is key in mantra meditation.

Chapter Eleven: Transcendental Meditation

Transcendental meditation is growing in influence and popularity as it is being incorporated into the programs of prisons, schools, and colleges in Europe, the US, Latin America, and India. What is so special about this form of meditation that is making various people practice it? You will find out in this chapter as we delve into what this meditation is all about, its benefit, and the way to practice it.

What is Transcendental Meditation?

This type of meditation was developed by Maharishi Mahesh Yogi. It is a silent meditation where you meditate to avoid distractions and attain a state of calmness and awareness. It is a meditation that can be practiced whether you are religious or not. It is a religious practice in Hinduism but you can practice it for the purpose of self-development if you are not religious. Transcendental meditation has been around for more than 50 years and it is endorsed by celebrities and various media outlets.

One of such celebrities that endorse transcendental meditation is Jonathan Rowson, the Scottish chess grandmaster. According to him, transcendental meditation offers you a feeling of balance, serenity, and energy. Other celebrities who practice this form of meditation regularly include Sam Allardyce, a football manager; Jennifer Aniston, an actress; Russell Brand, a stand-up comedian; and Ray Dalio, an investment banker. Therefore, if you choose to practice transcendental meditation, you are in good company.

Maharishi reckons that your thoughts are like bubbles that keep pouring in relentlessly like a stream. Hence, you need to be calm and aware to be able to have a proper thought. A proper thought is that thought that is devoid of sentiment and emotions. During the practice of transcendental meditation, you silently repeat mantras while seating comfortably. There is no specific posture or sitting position that you must assume before you can practice this type of meditation.

The mantra serves as a vehicle with which you evade noises in your mind and attain a quiet and calm state. The ordinary thinking process becomes transcended and replaced by a state of unadulterated consciousness. Every mental boundary is depleted and you will be able to attain a state of tranquility and orderliness.

Benefits of Practicing Transcendental Meditation

According to Dr. Norman E. Rosenthal, an award-winning psychiatrist from Georgetown University, if transcendental meditation can be put into a capsule and sold like a pharmaceutical product, it would have been a billion-dollar blockbuster! A remarkable statement, isn't it? Why will these celebrities and much more practice transcendental meditation if it is pointless? Definitely, there are benefits attached to the practice of this type of meditation. Do you care to know? Here they are:

Peak Performance

Many people have wondered what exactly makes transcendental meditation unique. One of the uniqueness of this form of meditation is that it aids the performance level of the practitioners. How? When you practice this meditation, the whole of your brain is turned on to function properly as a unit. A study in 2005 by Chandler and his colleagues on the effect of transcendental meditation technique on cognitive stage development revealed that regular practice of transcendental meditation enhances brain function. Therefore, don't be surprised that athletes with top performances and top businessmen and women are practicing transcendental meditation.

Reduction of Stress and Anxiety

The regular practice of transcendental meditation brings about a reduction in stress and anxiety. A study in the Harvard Medical School on the effect of transcendental meditation on cardiovascular function by Vernon Barnes and his colleagues in 2001 confirms that transcendental meditation reduces stress and anxiety.

Enhancement of Cardiovascular Health

In 2007, Anderson and his colleagues carried out a study to investigate the effect of transcendental meditation on blood pressure. The result of the study showed that transcendental meditation practices boost cardiovascular health.

Prevention and reduction of Depression

Depression is a major issue in the world today. The pressure to perform is on the rise and many people find it difficult to get to grips with the loss of their jobs and confidence in modern times. Transcendental meditation has proven to be a remedy and preventive measure against depression. A study on the treatment of Post Traumatic Stress Disorder (PTSD) by Boyd and his colleagues in 2013 has confirmed that the practice of transcendental meditation can remedy depression.

Prevention and Treatment of Addiction

Drug abuse is a malaise the government of different countries are doing all they can to fight against. However, people who practice transcendental meditation consistently does not have to worry about being infected by this "virus". Your general mood improves when you practice this form of meditation and you won't need any chemical substance to make you happy.

Treatment of Sleeplessness

You will not be able to perform up to the maximum level when your sleep is not regular. However, you don't have to worry about issues with sleepless when you are a consistent practitioner of transcendental meditation. The effect of transcendental meditation on sleeplessness is not a farce but a fact backed up with scientific evidence. One of the numerous studies that confirm the effect of transcendental meditation on sleeplessness was carried out in 2014 by Charles Elder and his colleagues. This study revealed that consistent transcendental meditation practice is effective against insomnia.

How to Practice Transcendental Meditation

For the best transcendental meditation, you will need a qualified and experienced transcendental meditation teacher. Such a teacher must be certified by the Maharishi Foundation, a non- profit organization recognized by the government of the United States of America. However, you can still practice on your own if you want to. To practice transcendental meditation, below are some useful tips:

Set out Time to Meditate

The best transcendental meditation practice requires you to practice at least twice a day. An average of twenty minutes each is good enough to practice. You have to ensure you are consistent to enjoy the full benefits of practicing this type of meditation.

Sit Comfortably in a Serene Environment

"Serenity" is relative when it comes to the practice of transcendental meditation. What matters is that you are in an environment that is comfortable for you to practice. Avoid practicing in a place where you will have to fight the thoughts going through your mind and external stimuli. Practice in a place where there is a level of noise that is acceptable for you so that you can focus. It is hard enough to focus during meditation. You don't need to make it further difficult for yourself. You can either sit on the ground or on a chair. What matters is for you to sit comfortably such that you don't strain your body or too relaxed such that you feel like sleeping.

Take a Few Deep Breaths

Take a few deep breaths while closing your eyes to keep you calm and release tension. Ensure you don't strain your body. Observe if there is tension in a part of your body especially the muscles of your face. Let go and relax to delve into a full meditative state.

Open your Eyes and Close Them Back Again

You will have to close your eyes all through the time of the practice. Hence, before you start muttering a mantra, you can close your eyes for the last time before you finally close them again to concentrate all through the period of the meditation.

Mutter a Mantra Repeatedly

A mantra is the anchor point on which you will focus all through the period of the practice. To enjoy a full experience of transcendental meditation, you should use a Sanskrit sound given to you by a certified transcendental meditation teacher.

The mantra for meditation in this form of meditation is not just a random positive mantra; it has to be a mantra whose energy and vibrations are endorsed by experts. This specific use of specially designed mantras is what makes the practice of transcendent meditation different from other forms of meditation.

Focus on the Mantra

Pay attention to the mantra all through the period of the practice. Your mind will wander off into a series of thoughts but you have to gently bring it back to the mantra. Your mind is prone to distraction and that impairs your performance in your daily activities. The practice if transcendental meditation enables you to train your mind to focus on what you want it to focus on. Don't fight it or feel bad about your mind drifting away, just calmly bring it back to the anchor point.

Ease yourself back to the World

Once you are done with the meditation, ease yourself back to the world by slowly moving your fingers and toes. Then open your eyes as you complete the meditation and enjoy the inner peace you have because of the meditation.

Other Important Tips

I believe you should also find the following tips useful to help you to practice transcendental meditation effectively:

Set an alarm to know when to stop meditating. You cannot afford any form of distraction while meditating. Hence, it is not ideal to check time to find out if you have meditated long enough. You may also assume that you have meditated for 20 minutes when you have only meditated for 5 minutes. You don't need that feeling of disappointment, just set an alarm to know when your time is up.

Don't forget that you should not access your performance while meditating but after meditating. There should not be any other thought occupying your mind all through the period of the practice apart from the mantra you are muttering. Strive for perfection as much as you can but ensure you do that before or after the meditation.

You can still practice transcendental meditation without getting a particular mantra from a transcendental meditation teacher. You can simply use "Homm" because it is a universal mantra used by monks for the practice of meditation. You can also use "Kirim" or "Shirim". Mutter them slowly to intentionally drag the pronunciation. I mean something like "Kiiiiiiriiiiiiiim" or "Shiiiiiiiiiriiiiiiiiiiiiiiiiiiiiim".

The most important thing about the practice of transcendental meditation is not the muttering of the mantra but to achieve inner peace and ease off stress. The idea is to transcend your mind by focusing on a meaningless word. Hence, if you notice that the mantra you are using sounds like a world you are familiar with, change it because it can distract you in the long run.

Chapter Twelve: Guided Meditation

We all need guidance in life. If you don't want to practice meditation by yourself because you want to be absolutely sure that you are doing it correctly, guided meditation is for you. Guided meditation? You don't need to be worked up about what it is all about and how you can practice it or what you stand to gain by practicing this type of meditation. You will get every answer you need in this chapter. You are about to be guided to meditate!

What is Guided Meditation?

This is a form of meditation in which you are guided by an experienced and qualified meditation teacher. Guided meditation takes away the burden of learning how to go about meditation. Your teacher will guide you through to know the best meditation posture and breathing exercise that will enable to practice effectively. You will not also need to worry about the mantra you can use during meditation because your teacher has got your back.

Your teacher does not necessarily have to be physically present with you during the meditation. The advancement in technology has broken the barrier of distance in learning. You can learn anything from a teacher at the comfort of your home including meditation. Hence, your learning may be through a video or podcast. Whether it is physically or via a video, you will be provided with each step you need and techniques as well as tips for meditation.

All you have to be concerned about is paying attention and practicing what you are taught. Guided meditation is recommended for beginners to enable you to explore and enjoy the full experience of meditation. You may be frustrated if you are trying so hard and you can see the benefit you expected to enjoy from the practice of meditation. Instead of reducing your stress level, you will end up increasing it. When you are not getting it right, meditation can often feel like buying a machine without a manual. You can practice on your own later after receiving guidance as you take your first steps on your journey of meditation.

Benefits of Practicing Guided Meditation

Unguided meditations are beneficial and guided meditations are not different. Below are the benefits of guided meditation:

Perfect for Meditation Beginners

Guided meditation is perfect for you if you are just trying to get to grips with meditation practices generally. Your first steps are important because they go a long way in determining your perception of meditation. If you don't have the right guidance when you are just starting to learn to meditate, you may assume that meditation is a worthless practice not worth your time. Hence, guided meditation ensures that you learn without experimentation.

Assurance and Confidence of Being on the Right Path

One of the greatest battle people who practice meditation by themselves have is the evaluation of how well they are practicing. Some people get distracted by the thought of whether they are practicing correctly or not while meditating. Guided meditation eliminates any worry about meditating correctly. You are learning from experts and you can rest assured in their rich experience and expertise.

Enhanced Calmness

Any form of meditation will make you comfortable and calm. However, it is better when you are meditating with the aid of a guide. You are sure that you are practicing correctly because of the credibility of your guide. Hence, you will be able to find it easier to delve into a full meditative state. Your mind and body is at peace with one another and you can focus on your breath or mantra easily. Every form of meditation makes you calm by taking your mind off your monkey mind and making it focus either on a mantra, your breath, or absolutely nothing. Guided takes this ability to focus a notch higher due to the fact that you have a definite and trusted guide.

Focus

Just like other forms of meditation, guided meditation enables you to retain your focus. The importance of focus cannot be overemphasized in your daily activities. The U.S. Marines have embraced mindfulness because they realized that it helps them to focus better on the job. If a credible organization like the U.S. Marine sees meditation as a helpful practice for enhanced focus, then, you are in good company when you choose to meditate consistently.

Prevention and Cure of Depression and Chronic Pain

You will not have reasons to bother about depression when you practice guided meditation. If you are already suffering from depression, it is not too late because guided meditation is also a remedy to depression. Psychologists from the University of Exeter recommend meditation as a cure for depression. They reckon that mindfulness is a better cure than drugs. According to their study, patients who practiced meditation for four months were better enough such that they did not need antidepressants again.

Prevention and Cure of Chronic Pain

According to a study conducted in the Wake University in 2011 by Fadel Zeidan and his colleagues, meditation was found to offer both preventive and curative effects to pain. In the study, the brain of the participants who practiced meditation was scanned with MRI. The scans revealed that there was a 40 percent reduction in pain! Therefore, instead of spending money on treating chronic pain like many people today, your lot can be far better with the consistent practice of meditation.

How to Find a Guide

In guided meditation, your guide will help you understand how your mind works as well as meditation techniques. You will know what to expect and how to go about it exactly. I don't need to give you steps on how to go about practicing guided meditation. What you need is a guide and you will get every step you need and more. How can you get someone to guide you? You can find a guide through the following ways:

Find a Local Meditation Class

By searching online with the aid of Google, you can find local meditation classes around you. There are many people like you around you who know the importance of meditation and are committed to practicing it. These people meet regularly and you can also join them. These groups are led by an expert who gives the requisite instructions and guidance for effective meditation. The style of meditation that will be practiced in a particular group depends on the teacher. Hence, you can find another group if you find it difficult to cope with the approach of the teacher of a particular group.

Download an Instructional App

If you are not comfortable with meditating in a group or for the sake of comfort, you can get an instructional app that will guide you. Search online for a tested and trusted digital app you can use. Ensure you read the reviews of previous users of the app before you download it. There are many people out there waiting to pounce on the ignorance of naïve people. So, you need to be careful. Instructional apps contain audios and videos of experts who will guide you on how to go about meditating. They provide you with techniques and other details you need to help you meditate effectively.

Online Music Services

Streaming music services like Spotify or Apple Music comes in handy when it comes to access to guided meditation sessions. All you need to do is to subscribe and you will gain access to guided meditation sessions of various lengths and practice styles.

Podcasts

Podcasts also provide you with guided meditation sessions that can be beneficial to you in various ways. Some podcasts provide you with information about meditation and its benefits while some will give you steps on how to practice it. Hence, regardless of your purpose of meditation, you will find podcasts beneficial. Without leaving your room or any other designated place where you can practice without distractions, you can practice with ease.

Websites

There are several mindfulness websites that offer you free guided meditations. Just search for such websites online and you will find a couple of credible ones. You will find guided meditations in both visual and audio formats in these sites.

YouTube

You can also get qualitative and quantitative guided meditations on YouTube and other video websites. These kinds of sites are the best for you if your preference is visual guided meditation sessions.

Other Important Tips

On the flip side, your decision to go for a teacher may be a result of low self-esteem which will not be good. If you just don't want to bother about the complexities or complications around meditation, guided meditation is a good choice. However, you can try to meditate by yourself first and then get a guide later. Compare the benefits of both before you finally make a decision. There is no scientific evidence that proves that you are better off with guided meditation.

Consider shorter sessions when you are just starting especially if you are not practicing with a physically available teacher. In other words, if you practicing with the aid of podcasts or YouTube videos, start with shorter sessions so that you can build your confidence and expertise steadily. You will do yourself a lot of good by switching off your phone or putting in on airplane mode when you want to meditate. You don't need any form of distraction in order to get the best out of guided meditation.

Don't procrastinate because you will never be consistent and enjoy the full dividends of meditation when you procrastinate. Set out time that is convenient for you and once that time comes, don't postpone it until some other time. The best time to meditate is now! Yes! Now!

Since meditation helps you to focus and get better sleep, it is better to practice it early in the morning to start the day on the right note or in the evening to make you relaxed to sleep well.

Avoid overconfidence because you are practicing guided meditation. Ensure you thoroughly scrutinize the credibility of your guide. All that glitters is not gold. Before you commit to a guide, ensure it is the right one.

Every form of meditation requires practice. Hence, don't think that guided meditation is some kind of shortcut. You will have to practice consistently to get the best out of any form of meditation you choose.

Chapter Thirteen: Dynamic Flow/Meditation in Motion

One indisputable fact about human beings is that we are not the same. The uniqueness of humans can be seen in our choice of food, spouse, dress sense, among other intricacies. Human uniqueness also spills into our choice of meditation type. Most of the type of meditation I have discussed so far involves sitting in a comfortable position. However, some people cannot imagine themselves doing that. They want to meditate but they are too "active" to meditate while sitting still.

You will not be the first person if you think meditation is not for such people. However, such people can also practice meditation. That should be good news for you if you are one of such people. Dynamic flow/meditation in motion is the perfect type of meditation for such people. All you need to know about this form of meditation and its practice are available in this chapter.

What is Dynamic Flow/Meditation in Motion?

This form of meditation emphasizes movement while attaining calmness. It was created by Osho (Bhagwan Shree Rajneesh), an Indian mystic sage. Osho believes that the modern world will benefit more from a meditation style that involves physical activities. He proposes over 100 meditation techniques that can be employed in the practice of this form of meditation. Dynamic flow meditation has stages but the end is to give you calmness and awareness.

Meditation in motion is not rigid as it does not have any particular method of practice. The flexibility of this type of meditation is one of the reasons it is gaining grounds in recent times. This method of meditation totally changes the perception of meditation as a practice meant for only monks who sit is a calm state in silence. Dynamic meditation brings a sense of "fun" to meditation which makes it attractive and exciting.

There is nothing weird about dynamic flow meditation because it is built on the core principles of meditation generally. Though there are many benefits of various forms of meditation, the three primary benefits are awareness of the present moment, focus, and calmness. The practice of meditation in motion offers you these three benefits and more. Hence, there is nothing to worry about because this form of meditation is not inferior in any way to other forms of meditation.

Tai chi and Kundalini yoga have the ingredients of dynamic flow meditation. Tai chi is a martial art that is based on the mind-body connection. The core principle of Tai chi is to create a balance between the forces of Yin and Yang. These are two opposing forces in the universe that needs to be in balance for you to be healthy. Tai chi involves movement, meditation, and deep breathing which are the core principles of dynamic flow meditation.

Kundalini yoga is a blend of chanting, mindfulness, and expression of power and energy. When you practice Kundalini yoga correctly, you will feel as though you have gone to the gym, gone for therapy, and had fun singing with friends at the same time. You stand to enjoy these same benefits when you practice meditation in motion.

Benefits of Dynamic Flow/Meditation in Motion

It is important you are aware of the things you stand to enjoy when you practice dynamic flow meditation. These benefits will spur you on to practice consistently especially during times when you are stressed out. Below are the benefits of practicing meditation in motion:

Calmness, Awareness, and Focus

Just like other forms of meditation, dynamic meditation offers you calmness and leaves you in a relaxed state. The fact that it involves movement makes it sound impossible but at the end of the practice of this form of meditation, you will enjoy an amazing state of calmness. Your awareness and focus are also heightened when you practice this type of meditation.

Reduction of Stress Level, Tension

The physical activity involved in dynamic flow meditation ensures that your blood circulation is enhanced. There will be more oxygen in your bloodstream and the front of your heart and spine will open up. The resultant effect of the enhanced blood circulation is that your stress level will reduce and you will be able to release tension.

Loads of Fun

Meditation in motion is fun and that ensures that you will not have issues with depression. This form of meditation heals your body and mind. You will be energized and feel alive and aware of your world. Dynamic flow meditation is a complete package of health benefits and fun.

How to Practice Dynamic Flow/Meditation in Motion

Practicing meditation in motion is not difficult. Like I have said earlier, there is no particular method you have to follow to practice this form of meditation. However, just like every other form of meditation, you need to schedule the meditation and find somewhere conducive enough for you to practice. Apart from these, below are the steps you can follow to practice meditation in motion:

Get Enough Space

It is not just good enough to find a place that is comfortable in the sense of serenity, it is more important you get enough space. Remember that you need space to move around while meditating; hence, ensure you choose a place where you can move without inhibition. Once you are restricted during meditation in motion, you cannot get the best out of this type of meditation because it is not a sitting meditation.

Begin by Breathing Slowly through Your nose

The practice of dynamic flow meditation begins by breathing slowly through your nose. Inhale and exhale slowly as air fill your lungs and leave them. You need to master these slow deep breaths because it is the foundation upon which this form of meditation is built. All through the period of meditation, you will have to take deep breaths.

Slightly increase the Pace of your Breaths for Ten Minutes

After the initial phases when you take breathe slowly, you will increase the pace and breathe faster for ten minutes. Focus on thorough exhalation and inhalation. You will continue to breathe faster but you must ensure that you continue to take deep breaths. Breathe deeply into your lungs and exhale completely before the next breath without reducing the pace. It may not be easy initially but you will master it by practice. The essence of this breathing pattern is to make you lose track of the sensations in your body while breathing.

Move in an Uncoordinated Manner

If you think the earlier steps have been boring, things are about to get more interesting now. The next phase involves moving chaotically. You can be creative about the way you go about this stage. You can choose to jump, dance, laugh out loud, or scream. The essence of these uncoordinated movements is so that you will further lose track of your body by creating a catharsis for your body. Don't forget to continue with the deep breaths while moving around without paying attention to the pattern of movement.

Raise your Arms above your Head

You are going to settle for a pattern now after the uncoordinated movement phase. You will start by raising your arms above your head.

Jump Up and Down as you Shout "Hoo!"

With your arms still raised above your head, jump up and down and shout "hoo!" each time. Each time you land on your feet, you will feel your feet sending a vibration through the center of your body. Savor this sensation without stopping the jump. Continue like this for ten minutes before you move to the next stage.

Stop Moving and Stay in a Position for 15 minutes

Freeze in a position and pay attention to what is happening to your body. You have created positive energy in your body through the earlier activities and you should feel it. The essence of this is to train your mind to be aware of the moment and enjoy it. Continue taking deep breaths while doing this. The recommendation of Osho meditation is that you should not move at all during this phase. You are completely in charge and you are savoring every sensation going on in your body during this stage.

Celebrate for 15 Minutes

The climax of dynamic flow meditation is the last phase when you celebrate your progress. Meditation in motion is such that you don't have to celebrate your progress later but within the meditation. Do whatever you do when you are in a happy mood at the end of the meditation. You can laugh, dance, run around, or sing. The essence of this meditation is not just to celebrate your progress but to let go of your body in an excited state.

Other Important Tips

I am convinced that the steps to follow to practice meditation in motion as highlighted above are straightforward. Below are other tips that can aid effective practice:

There is no method of meditation that is superior or inferior. It is all about what you feel is best for you. Hence, if you practice meditation in motion and it suits you, why not? However, if you prefer a meditation style where you sit still, stick with it. Never practice a method of meditation just because people around it practice it.

As a beginner, you can reduce the recommended minutes to half and increase it with time. You are permitted to have your own abbreviated version initially but you must ensure you get better over time.

Don't allow anyone to discourage you. What you are doing may not make sense to people who have not experienced the power of meditation before. Focus on what you need to do and critics will end up asking you to teach them later when they see your progress as a result of regular practice.

Meditation in motion is a physical exercise. Hence, don't forget to wear flexible clothing and shoes with soft soles that can support you when you jump. A towel and water around you is a good idea so that you can look after your body immediately after the meditation.

Chapter Fourteen: Prayer, Even if You are Not Religious

When you hear "prayer", it is likely that what comes to your mind that it is a sacred activity that people who are involved in one religion or the other carry out. However, you don't have to be religious before you can pray. Are you surprised? I am glad if I am the first person to tell you. What do you have to pay me for that? A lot of attention in this chapter! You will learn how to pray in this chapter even if you are not a religious person.

Changing your World with your Thoughts

You are not the only one if what prayer meant to you is clasping your hands and asking a deity to grant you your heart desire. Some people stopped believing in religion when they realize that people who are not religious are enjoying the same things they ask a deity to grant them. The right mindset is more important than cowering before a deity to grant your desires. I am not in any way saying that religion is obsolete.

However, you need to know that there is so much you can do with your mind without any religious affiliation. In other words, the only time you pray is not when you are reciting "Our Father" (Christianity) or "Mrityunjaya Mantra (Hinduism). In other words, you can be spiritual without any religious affiliation.

According to Dr. Brian Weiss:

"One way to raise your vibration is to fill your heart and mind with loving-kindness, with tranquility, and with peace. When you can create and manifest such an energy field, your burdens will be eased, even in the toughest of times."

You can connect with your "Higher Power" through prayer without beseeching a deity. You need to change your perception about prayer if you have always only seen it in a religious way. It is high time you saw prayer as an activity that enables you to align your thoughts and strengthen your energy. The result of prayer is that it enables you to have the right thoughts and make the right decisions. You get guidance to go in a particular direction or talk to someone or say something that will make a positive difference in your life.

Affirmative Prayer

Affirmative prayer involves setting your heart to the possibility of something positive happening and affirming it with your words. Your thoughts create vibrations that go out into the world. Your thoughts have the capacity to create situations. You are a powerful creator and there is no limitation to what you can do when you align your thoughts with your dreams. Hence, you have to avoid filling your mind with negative thoughts.

You can experience the energy of people be it positive or negative when you are around them. You can know someone who is in a bad mood even before the person speaks to you because the state of the person's mind radiates energy. In the same way, you can tell when a person is in a good mood because of the kind of vibration the state of their mind produces. Hence, you radiate energy with your thoughts and this energy may be creative or destructive. The energy you radiate can work against you or work for you.

You can take advantage of prayer to ease your burdens and calm yourself down without necessarily believing in a deity. When you think about something and affirm it with your words in prayer. You will be surprised that circumstances arrange themselves and your request is somehow granted. You will ride on the ripple effect of the energy you created by praying and meet people who can help you achieve or find what you want.

Tips on Praying Without Being Religious

To create your own spiritual pathway with prayer, below are some helpful tips to pray without a religious affiliation:

Meditate

Meditation provides you serenity and calmness of mind. You can have your own sacred place where you meditate and connect to your higher self. You can choose any form of meditation and practice it regularly to regulate the thoughts of your mind and be at peace with yourself. You can create somewhere in your house and make it sacred to you. A place you go to unburden your stress and lose yourself in a meditative state and create positive energy.

Be Grateful

Nothing creates more negative energy than a hurting or bitter heart. It will prevent you from seeing the positive things happening around you and kill every sense of optimism. However, if you think deeply enough, you will realize that you have many reasons to be grateful in spite of the challenges and difficulties you are going through. When you practice meditation, you will be able to have a better perception of your life. You may not have money but you have people around you who love you. Be grateful for the relationship you have and the gift of life. Make it a daily practice to take out like fifteen minutes to deliberately find reasons to be grateful in your life. Reflection and gratitude will enable you to connect with your spiritual self and find comfort money cannot buy.

Enjoy the Moment

There are many things around you that are wonderful and lovely but you will never pay attention to them when you are not aware of the moment. Walk in the woods when you are not busy in the evening and just admire the beauty of nature. Enjoy the ambience of the moment and appreciate the beauty of something greater than you. Look at how vast the earth is and how it supports life. Secular spirituality is all about enjoying the moment and refusing to get lost in negative thoughts. Become alive and aware as you create positive energy around you with your thoughts. Prayer goes beyond just making requests. Create positive vibes with pure positive thoughts and words and create a comfortable atmosphere to attract the right people and the right circumstances to yourself. Don't allow whatever you change about your life cannot overwhelm you. Let the thoughts of possibilities about the things you can change in your life consume your thoughts.

Look Within

You can easily drift such that you value yourself on the basis of the things happening around you. However, your true worth lies with you. Only you can know what you are worth. There is no great person today who has not been misjudged and deemed useless by people at one point of their lives. Hence, it is your choice to either see yourself as a worthless person or a person of worth. People will learn to see the true you and appreciate your qualities over time. However, your voice will never be heard when you drown in the thoughts of the negative things people have said about you. Focus on your strength and work on improving areas where you are not strong.

Keep a Journal

You can take things a notch higher by writing down your thoughts in your personal journal. Don't just write down random thoughts that come to your mind. Filter your thoughts and write down the positive things you think about yourself. There is no amount of appreciation or acceptance you can get from people that can rival your appreciation and acceptance of yourself. Ensure you keep your evaluation of yourself honest. Begin by writing about the qualities you have and smile all the way as you write. Then, move on to writing down areas where you need to improve. Don't stop there; write out practical ways with which you can improve on your deficiencies. The best time to do this is after meditation when you mind is calm and your thoughts are fully under your control.

Listen to Music

Listening to songs that resonate with you helps you to create positive vibes around you. Meditate on the lyrics and appreciate the creativity that has produced the song. Enjoy the tune and notice the tempo as well as the musical instruments used to create the work. Appreciate the symphony and the beautiful synchronization of the singing and the musical instruments. Music has the ability to move people to tears or create a state of elation. It is a vehicle that can connect you to your higher self with ease.

Practice Empathy

Having an awareness of the struggles and pains of people around you connects you spiritually to them. Practicing loving-kindness meditation gives you a head start in connecting with people around you. Don't just think about what they are going through; seek how to alleviate them of their pain. You will be able to attain inner peace every time you make the choice to lift up others. We all need ourselves and the height of spirituality is to live for the common good. Religion without love stinks and it is hypocritical. We are not designed for isolation but a community where love is the watchword.

Create Rituals

You need a routine if you are serious about your spiritual life. You must create time for your personal growth. You can do the dish while keeping an eye on the birds having a jolly ride in the sky outside your window. Be creative about your ritual. The most important thing is to do something that takes your mind away from your worry about debt or work or other things that makes you stressed. Just live every moment and be fully aware of what is going on around you.

Celebrate Life

Activities such as running in nature can give you a spiritual connection with the universe. Running in nature is a physical exercise that has both physical and spiritual benefits. Celebrating in a healthy body ease you of tension and makes you feel alive. During holiday celebrations, say words that show you are grateful for your life and the beauty in it. Be the best version of yourself every day by creating positive energy with spiritual activities. You don't have to go to parties and get drunk or have sex before you can feel elated and alive. It is the absence of a culture of practicing spirituality that makes people seek such unprofitable alternatives.

Chapter Fifteen: How to Establish a Consistent Meditation Practice

When you see people who practice meditation regularly, you will admire them. They look younger than their age, full of life, and have no worries. They are on top of their game in their daily activities with an incredible level of awareness and focus. They live life to the fullest with a moment-by-moment approach that makes them buzz with positive energy.

Such people are not freaks but regular people who have made the choice to commit and dedicate their time to practice meditation come day come shine. They are good role models and you can also follow in their footsteps. I know one or two things that help people to maintain a consistent meditation practice. Here are a few things I believe can also help you on your journey to practice meditation consistently:

Find People of Like Minds

You need the right company to achieve anything in life. Whether you believe it or not, you are a product of the influence of people. These people may be close to you or far away from you but you definitely have people whose actions or inactions influence your decision. You may not be able to realize quickly until you think and trace where the influence came from. In fact, your decision to read this book on meditation is a product of the influence of someone or some people on you. There is nothing wrong with having people who inspire you or influence you as long as they are leading you in the right direction.

The journey is smoother when you have someone you can discuss your success and failure with. Hence, if you want to be consistent in your practice of meditation, you need people of like minds. You need people who believe in the power of meditation and are also willing to or are already practicing consistently. When you have someone you are accountable to, things become easier. It is easier especially when you and the person meditate at the same time and at the same place. You know that the person will ask why you did not come around and that alone will keep you on your toes to be consistent.

Never forget that the Benefits of Meditation is only for the Consistent

I have mentioned many benefits of meditation so far in this book. I am convinced that you will like to enjoy these benefits too. However, meditation is not something you can just do and stop whenever you feel like. You have to be committed to it to enjoy the benefits. Since you want to enjoy these benefits; you should also maintain a committed attitude towards practicing it. If you keep reminding yourself that it is only with consistent practice that you can reap the benefits of meditation, you will have enough motivation to practice consistently.

It is just like trying to lose weight and not willing to be committed to your regiment. Such a person will not be able to achieve any reasonable result. Meditation can even help you lose weight as backed up by scientific evidence which I have explained earlier. If you have the right tool in your hands, then, you should not let anything stop you from using it consistently for your own benefit.

Practice Every Morning

As much as you can actually practice meditation at any time of the day, it is better you practice it early in the morning for the sake of consistency. In the morning, you are still fresh especially if you have had a good night's rest. You still have enough energy to practice and enjoy the meditation. Besides, you will have enough calmness and focus that will help you record peak performance for the rest of the day. By the time you go into the day and you are encumbered by the stress of the day, you may find it difficult to practice again. Hence, unless it is absolutely impossible, ensure you practice meditation early in the morning so that you can be more consistent. That does not mean that you will not enjoy the benefits of consistent meditation at other times of the day. However, you will open your path to consistent practice with an early morning meditation.

Connect it with an Activity you do daily

I doubt there is any day you don't brush your teeth. You don't want to even imagine how your breath will be when you don't brush your teeth for just a day. I am sure you are even uncomfortable with the fact that I called it "just a day". Most people will lose their confidence and will keep a distance from other people when they speak if they have not brushed their teeth that day. Mind you, when you meditate, you are not only taking care of your body but primarily your mind. See meditation daily as "washing your mind daily". It may sound funny but that is exactly what you are doing.

You are taking charge of your mind and "washing" away negative thoughts and sensations. Hence, don't just feel uncomfortable when you have not brushed your teeth in a day, you should also feel uncomfortable when you have not meditated away. Remember that one meditation per day keeps the medical doctor, psychologists, and psychiatrist far away from you. Consistent meditation indirectly reduces your bills because you will have fewer reasons to pay physical and psychological health practitioners.

Use the Same Time and Place

It is good to experiment with different times and places when you are a beginner so that you can know what works best for you. However, you have to find the best time and place for you quickly so that you can settle and practice consistently. Chopping and changing your meditation time and location consistently will not make you consistent. Your practice of meditation has to be a routine – a ritual. Your mind and body must get used to that time and location such that it almost becomes a reflex action. Meditation must move from one of your activities and become a permanent habit. You need to be consistent with the timing and place where you meditate to make this possible. Once it becomes your habit, you will become "addicted" to it. Meditation is a positive addiction that kicks out negative addictions.

Don't Let Guilt Stop you

It is good that you make yourself feel uncomfortable with missing your meditation every morning. You should be your own best critic and should not allow yourself to lose your discipline. However, if it happened that you missed it one morning; ensure that you make up for it in the evening. Don't fall into the trap of feeling so bad because you missed your meditation in the morning such that you skip it altogether.

In the same way, if things got so bad that you missed your meditation all day long (it should never happen!), don't decide to quit altogether because of guilt. You may miss your meditation a day or two when you are just starting because your body is trying to get used to it. Make you encourage yourself to continue. You stand so much to gain from consistent meditation practice. Hence, don't allow anything to stop you; not even guilt!

Don't Be Too Hard on Yourself

Self-evaluation is good because it enables you to measure your progress. However, you need to avoid being too critical of yourself as regards whether you are good or bad in meditation. Judge your progress on the basis of your consistency. In other words, you should feel bad when you are not practicing consistently and double up on time. However, when it comes to the actual practice of meditation, you need to avoid being judgmental. Remember that various forms of meditation exist and most are flexible. Hence, if you are practicing consistently, you will reap the benefits. I don't mean that you should not seek new and better ways to improve your effectiveness in meditation. However, let your primary basis of evaluation be your consistency.

Be Realistic About your Expectation

I need to say it loud and clear that meditation is not a magic wand that will take away all your problems. In the long run, you can attain financial independence through consistent meditation practice. How? If your parents don't own the oil wells in Saudi Arabia or a business empire, you know you have to work hard to attain financial independence. The decisions you make every day, as well as your focus on your goal, will determine whether you will succeed or not. Consistent meditation practice enables you to have a still mind such that you can make consistent quality decisions. Quality decision making can, in the long run, enable you to achieve your dream.

However, you should not practice meditation consistently as a means to earn wealth. It does not directly make you prosperous. There are various factors including unforeseen circumstances that contribute to your success or failure. Hence, practice meditation for the immediate rewards of a calm mind, awareness, and focus. Other indirect benefits can come in later but you have to be realistic. If you have an undue expectation of what you stand to enjoy from the practice of meditation, you will be disappointed in the short run and may even quit. Hence, if you want to be consistent in your practice of meditation, your focus must be on the short-term gain first. Just enjoy meditating daily and enjoy each day as it comes.

Keep an Excuse Book

An excuse book is a book where you write down the reason you did not do what you have planned to do. In this case, keep an excuse book where you write down why you did not meditate in case you missed out on any day. You will not want to keep writing excuses that remind you of your ineptitude. Hence, it will spur you on to practice consistently.

Chapter Sixteen: Stages of the Path

Meditation is a journey; a path that leads to may promising destinations. It is a path that leads you to find your spirituality and a path to self-discovery. It is a journey that will help you develop various aspects of your life. In this last chapter, I will help you with practical tips on how you can develop your emotions, senses, relationships, career, and your personal life as well as dharma via consistent meditation practice.

Emotions

According to the Eco Institute, consistent practice of meditation boosts your emotional quotient (EQ). In other words, when you practice meditation consistently, you will be able to manage your emotions effectively. Emotional intelligence is a big deal. Emotional intelligence refers to the ability to manage your emotions and the emotions of people around you effectively. It is not only negative emotions that you have to manage effectively but also positive emotions too! In fact, you need to be more careful about managing positive emotions because you normally want them to run wide.

Negative emotions are easy to spot and they don't make you comfortable with yourself and you will want to snap out of them as soon as possible. However, you want to let yourself loose when you are elated because something pleasant happened to you. You can feel on top of the world such that you begin to feel you don't need anybody in your life. Hence, you need meditation for both positive and negative emotions.

Emotions exist in eight main forms which include love, sadness, anger, shame, disgust, jealousy, happiness, and fear. Other forms of emotions like defeat and bitterness are derivatives of these eight emotions. The most important factor when it comes to the development of your emotional intelligence is for you to be able to recognize the source of the emotion. Sometimes you feel so sad and you really don't know why you are feeling that way. There are also days when you feel extremely happy and glowing inside of you but you can't get hold of the source.

When you practice meditation, you will be able to have a clear and calm mind that helps you monitor your thinking pattern adequately. Consequently, you will be able to find out the source of your emotions. Once you locate the source of your emotions, you can easily diffuse it if it is a negative emotion or keep it at bay if it is a positive emotion.

Senses

It may sound ridiculous but you can also develop the use of your senses with consistent practice of meditation. What I mean by the good use of your senses is not as though you want to make them function properly but to use them to stay aware of your environment. You may be staring but seeing nothing without being blind. You can be smelling something but not perceiving any sensation. There is a way stress and anxiety can make you dumb. Your senses are working perfectly but you are not aware of what is happening around you.

You can be eating the most delicious meal in the world but not enjoy it. Meanwhile, someone else will be eating a meal that is not as palatable and nutritious as your meal and the person will be having a good time. Your emotions can mess up with the function of your senses. If you are troubled in your mind, you will be looking at things happening around you but nothing will be colorful. You will not be able to experience the beauty of life even when it is all around you.

Hence, you need to take charge of your mind so that you will be able to stay aware and conscious about your environment. When you practice meditation consistently, you will be able to have good use of your senses. You will not just stare at things but see the beauty of life and creativity around you. You will live in the moment and savor every aroma and taste gleefully. You will not just touch, you will feel. It all begins with your mind before your body can experience life to its fullest.

Relationships

Your relationship with the people around you is the most important treasure you have. What about money? You cannot have money without people and money is worthless without people. If you are a business owner, your relationship with your customers goes a long way in determining whether you will succeed in business or not. If you have happy customers, you will be happy because you will also smile to the bank. However, if your customers are not happy with you, you are going to lose your investment.

Apart from business, you must be able to have healthy relationships with various people in your life. You cannot live a happy and peaceful life if you are always at loggerheads with people around you. It is not possible to be in the good books of everyone but it is a serious problem when nobody wants to be around you. The way you manage and handle your emotions and the emotions of people around you is the foundation of healthy relationships. If you are easily irritable and intolerant, people will avoid you.

All hope is not lost if you have struggled with keeping friends because of your struggles with your emotions. The practice of a form of meditation like loving-kindness meditation can help you live in peace and harmony with yourself and the people around you. Meditation helps you to handle your emotions so that you can handle the emotions of people around you properly. When you are able to handle the emotions of people around you effectively, you will be able to maintain stable and healthy relationships consistently.

Work

I will only be wasting my time if I am trying to convince you about the importance of your work. For some people, their job is the most important part of their lives. The truth is that there is hardly anyone who will readily admit that their job is the most important part of their lives. However, you can know if your job is the most important thing for you when you find it easy to sacrifice your personal happiness and the family of your friends and family for your job.

You should be committed and dedicated to your job and give it your best. However, it should not be at the cost of your personal happiness and the happiness of people who matter or should matter to you the most. You should do all within your means to reach the peak of your career. If you are going to reach the peak of your career, you need these three important qualities: awareness, focus, and calmness.

You need to focus to achieve your dream and carry your team along as a leader. You need to be calm to remain productive and emotionally intelligent when you are under pressure. Calmness enables you to make quality decisions, especially during tough situations seamlessly. Awareness guarantees that you are in control and conscious of your environment and the people around you. It takes awareness to be empathetic towards others. Regular practice meditation offers you awareness, calmness, and focus which are three important qualities you need to succeed in your career.

Life

It will not be complete and proper if I talk about every other aspect of your life and fail to mention your personal life. Some people get it wrong by mixing their relationships and work with their personal life. It is true that you are designed to be a functional part of a community but you must never at any point lose your personal identity. You are a unique individual who needs to find expression. It is when you are personally healthy that you can contribute as an integral part of a team or a community.

Despite the fact that you will share a lot of things in common with your spouse, your personal identity and difference cannot diminish. Some people find marriage suffocating and end up pulling out because they lose themselves in the union. They feel lost, jaded, and out of sort. You must have activities you do regularly to keep your body and mind functioning properly. Meditation is an activity that is beneficial to you as a person. Your personal life needs positive generated with consistent practice.

Dharma

The teaching of Buddha is the "dharma" which is a pragmatic approach to life issues based on the development of the mind. It is a teaching that promotes the cultivation of a liberated and peaceful mind. This teaching encourages you to discover your personal truth which is practicable for you rather than pursuing speculative views in the name of faith. Dharma has to do with being free from cravings, complexities and any other form of complexities.

In the words of the Buddha:

"The Dharma is well proclaimed by the Blessed One; it is visible here and now, immediate, inviting to be seen for oneself, onward leading, and to be personally realized."

You are on a journey to self-discovery and further self-discovery which is a life-long journey. Your journey has a direction with a consistent practice of meditation.

Conclusion

We have finally come to the end of this incredible journey. I believe you thoroughly enjoyed the ride. Life is easier and enjoyable when you know what to do, how to do, and when to do it. If you were a complete novice before you started reading this book, I believe you have a clear idea about what meditation is all about now. You have a good grasp of what you stand to enjoy when you practice regularly and how you can practice.

I guess you must have been intrigued by the fact that there are numerous forms of meditation. However, you can actually summarize them into two distinct categories based on guidance: guided meditation and unguided meditation. Unguided meditations are all the forms of meditation I mentioned in this book apart from guided meditation. The variety of meditations available for you to practice shows that you don't have an excuse not to meditate.

If you prefer a form of meditation where you can have a semblance of monks, you can have your way. On the flip side, if you prefer a meditation that is kind of funky where you can move and groove, meditation in motion is available for you. Therefore, no matter your purpose for meditation or preference, there is always a form of meditation that suits you. Having taken your time to read through the different types of meditation and techniques, I believe you must have found one that suits you by now.

I believe you must have been impressed by the fact that meditation is not as rigid as most people think. You can always modify your meditation to suit your need for consistent practice. I have also deliberately gone for an evidence-based approach as regards the benefits of practicing meditation regularly. I notice that a couple of books about meditation out there stated the benefits without providing scientific evidence that supports their claims. It is okay to have your doubts because credibility is a serious issue in the modern world where a lot of people claim to be what they are not.

Some people wish that the benefits they expect to find through the practice of meditation are real. You don't need to bother about that because they are real. You are not the only one who is interested in the credibility of the claims that meditation offers consistent practitioners long life, stress reduction, calmness, awareness, and other benefits.

It will be a huge shame and a total waste of time if you took your time to read this book and you did not make a commitment to practice meditation consistently afterward. The essence of every chapter of this book until the last is to give you reasons why you should practice meditation every day. I have failed if I am not able to give you enough reasons to commit yourself to regular meditation practice. This is not one of the books you should read and forget about the information you have received.

I did not write this book to uncover anything mystical because there is nothing mystical about meditation. I have taken my time to research thoroughly to compile this material because I am convinced that your life will be better when you choose to commit to regular meditation. You know what meditation is all about now and you have also seen the benefits of practicing it which is based on empirical evidence. You have been exposed to the techniques involved and what you need to do to practice either guided or unguided meditation.

The ball is now left in your court to take advantage of this quality information and turn your life around. You have been equipped with the knowledge you need to live a happy and meaningful life through the practice of meditation consistently. You have a world to explore, opportunities to utilize, and people who need your contribution. I know you will make the right choice which is to begin or continue a regular practice of meditation. See you at the top of your game on top of your world.

I'd like to thank you and congratulate you for reading this book. I know you could have picked any number of books to read, but you picked this book and for that I am extremely grateful.

If you enjoyed this book and found some benefit in reading this, I'd like to hear from you and hope that you could take some time to post a review. Your feedback and support will help this author to greatly improve his writing craft for future projects and make this book even better.

I want you, the reader, to know that your review is very important and so, if you'd like to leave a review, all you have to do is post a review where you purchased this book. I wish you all the best in your future success!

Thank you and good luck!

Harini Anand

References

Anderson, N., Lau, M., Segal, Z., & Bishop, S. (2007). Mindfulness-based stress reduction

and attentional control. *Clinical Psychology & Psychotherapy*. 14. 449 - 463.

10.1002/cpp.544.

Barnes, V., & Treiber, F., & Davis, H. (2001). Impact of Transcendental Meditation(R)

on cardiovascular function at rest and during acute stress in adolescents with

high normal blood pressure. Journal of psychosomatic research. 51. 597-605.

10.1016/S0022-3999(01)00261-6.

Blacks, D., & Slavich, G. (2016). Mindfulness meditation and the immune system: a

systematic review of randomized controlled trials. *The New York Academy of*

Science. Doi: 10.1111/nyas.12998.

Blacks, D.S., O'Reilly, G.A., Olmstead R., Breen E.C., & Irvin M.R. (2015).

Mindfulness Meditation and Improvement in Sleep Quality and Daytime

Impairment Among Older Adults with Sleep Disturbances: A Randomized

Clinical Trial. *JAMA Intern Med* 175(4):494-501. Doi:

10.1001/jamainternmed.20148081.

Boyd, J. E., Lanius, R. A., & McKinnon, M. C. (2018). Mindfulness-based treatments for

posttraumatic stress disorder: A review of the treatment literature and

neurobiological evidence. *Journal of Psychiatry & Neuroscience, 43*(1), 7–

25. https://doi.org/10.1503/jpn.170021

Chandler, H.M., Alexander, C.N., & Heaton, D. (2005). The transcendental meditation

program and postconventional self-development: A 10-year longitudinal study.

Journal of Social Behavior and Personality. 17. 93-121.

Elder, C., Nidich, S., Moriarty, F., & Nidich. (2014). Effect of Transcendental Meditation

on Employee Stress, Depression, and Burnout: A Randomized Controlled Study.

The Permanente journal. 18. 19-23. 10.7812/TPP/13-102.

Gaiswinkler, L., Unterrainer, H.F. (2016). The relationship between yoga involvement,

mindfulness and psychological well-being. *Complementary Therapies in Medicine,*

26(1), 123-127. doi:10.1016/j.ctim.2016.03.011

Graser, L. & Stangier, U. (2018). Compassion and Loving-Kindness Meditation: An

Overview and Prospects for the Application in Clinical Samples.

Harvard Review of Psychiatry. 26. 201-215. 10.1097/HRP.0000000000000192.

Hacker, P., Davis, Jr., D.R. (2006). Dharma in Hinduism. *Journal of Indian Philosophy,*

34(5), 479-496. doi:10.1007/s10781-006-9002-4

Hatcher, B.A. (2007). Bourgeois Vedanta: The colonial roots of middle-class

Hinduism. *Journal of the American Academy of Religion, 75(2),* 298-323.

doi:10.1093/jaarel/lfm005

Lo P., & Tsai P., Kang H., & Tian W. (2018). Cardiorespiratory and autonomic-nervous-

system functioning of drug abusers treated by Zen meditation. Journal of

Traditional and Complementary Medicine. 9. 10.1016/j.jtcme.2018.01.005.

Lu, F., Xu, Y., Yu, Y., Wu, T., Liu, B., Xu, S., ... Li, M. (2019). Moderating Effect of

Mindfulness on the Relationships Between Perceived Stress and Mental Health

Outcomes Among Chinese Intensive Care Nurses. *Frontiers in Psychiatry*, 1664-

0640. Doi:10.3389/fpsyt.2019.00260.

Pagnoni G., Cekic M., & Guo Y. (2008). "Thinking about Not-Thinking": Neural

Correlates of Conceptual Processing during Zen Meditation. PloS one. 3. e3083.

10.1371/journal.pone.0003083.

Trousselard, M., Steiler, D., Claverie, D., & Canini, F. (2014). The history of Mindfulness

put to the test of current scientific data: Unresolved questions. *Encephale-Revue*

de Psychiatrie Clinique Biologique et Therapeutique, 40(6), 474-480.

doi:10.1016/j.encep.2014.08.006

Turakitwanakan, W., Mekseepralard, C., & Busarakumtragul, P. (2013). Effects of

mindfulness meditation on serum cortisol of medical students. *J Med Assoc Thai.*

96 Suppl 1. S90-5.

Woods-Giscombé, C. L., & Gaylord, S. A. (2014). The Cultural Relevance of Mindfulness

Meditation as a Health Intervention for African Americans: Implications for

Reducing Stress-Related Health Disparities. *Journal of holistic nursing : official*

journal of the American Holistic Nurses' Association, 32(3), 147–160.

doi:10.1177/0898010113519010

World Health Organization: WHO. (2018). Depression. Retrieved November 23, 2019,

from https://www.who.int/news-room/factsheets/detail/depression

Zeidan, F., Martucci, K., Kraft, R., Gordon, N., McHaffie, J., & Coghill, R. (2011). Brain

Mechanisms Supporting the Modulation of Pain by Mindfulness Meditation.

Journal of Neuroscience. 32. 5540.

Meditation Checklist

Use this simple checklist to make sure you have The Most Powerful Meditation Every Time

FIND OUT MORE

Made in the USA
Coppell, TX
01 July 2022

79443057R10080